Lazy- Bed

Gardening

The Quick and Dirty Guide

Lazy-Bed Gardening

The Quick and Dirty Guide

by

John Jeavons

and

Carol Cox

Ecology Action

Illustrations by Sue Ellen Parkinson

↑⊜ Ten Speed Press

TEN SPEED PRESS
P. O. Box 7123
Berkeley, California 94707

Much of the data and other information in this book has been drawn from *How to Grow More Vegetables* . . . 4th ed. by John Jeavons, Ten Speed Press, 1991.

Cover design by Nancy Austin

About the Boise Peace Quilters: On the cover of *Lazy-Bed Gardening* is a photograph of Quilt #19, awarded to John Jeavons in 1988. The Peace Quilters use needle and thread to create their art in recognition of significant contributions toward bringing peace to the world. Quilts have been exchanged with peacemakers in many countries. Among the other recipients are Dr. Helen Caldecott, Pete Seeger, and Senator Frank Church. For more information about the Peace Quilters, send a self-addressed stamped envelope to BOISE PEACE QUILT PROJECT, P.O. Box 6469, Boise, ID 83707.

Library of Congress Cataloging-in-Publication

Jeavons, John.
    Lazy-bed gardening / by John Jeavons and Carol Cox.
        p.   cm.
    Includes bibliographical references.
    ISBN 0-89815-452-9 : $8.95
     1. Vegetable gardening. 2. Biointensive gardening.
  3. Fruit—culture.   I. Cox, Carol.   II. Title.
  SB324.3.J44   1993
  635--dc20   91-37904
                                                      CIP

Lazy-Bed Gardening

CONTENTS

PREFACE

More than twenty years ago, Ecology Action published the first best-selling how-to book on high-yield, resource-conserving, biologically intensive food-raising techniques. At the time little was known about these "new" Biointensive methods, which are actually thousands of years old. We spent several years rediscovering these exciting practices and then shared them in *How To Grow More Vegetables Than You Ever Thought Possible On Less Land Than You Can Imagine.* Over one quarter of a million copies are now in print in five languages plus Braille. Ecology Action currently has thirty publications in use in 107 countries. Hundreds of other books and publications have drawn upon ours to include Biointensive techniques. Major regreening projects are underway in Mexico, Kenya, the Philippines, India and Russia.

The original *How To Grow More Vegetables* was a relatively simple book, and, as the years passed and we learned more, new editions were published by Ten Speed Press. Eventually, the thrust of the book became how to grow more *food* and emphasized the growing of calorie crops such as grains and beans, as well as fruits and nuts, herbs, flowers and even fiber crops. In the process the book became longer and a bit too technical for some, particularly beginning gardeners.

As a result, Ecology Action and Ten Speed Press decided that a simpler book should be written for those trying these methods for the first time, as well as for the seasoned gardener in need of streamlined information. *Lazy-Bed Gardening* is the result. This book is the distillation of twenty years of our own experience and the experiences of thousands of other gardeners around the world. We are delighted to be able to share it with you. Some technical information has been included, which can be bypassed easily if you do not need that level of detail. It is our hope that this book will make it easier for you to create "living soil" and a wonderful lush, vibrant mini-ecosystem in your own backyard -- or even your front yard -- resulting in an edible landscape that will provide you with fresh and stored food all through the year.

John Jeavons
Willits, California
January 15, 1993

ACKNOWLEDGEMENTS

Special thanks to:

- the people at Ten Speed Press -- Phil Wood, Publisher; George Young, Editor-in-Chief; Fuzzy, for all her administrative assistance; Nancy Austin, for graphic design; Brenton Beck of Fifth Street Design, for graphic design; Hal Hershey of Hal Hershey Book Design, for cover design; and Carolyn Miller, for extraordinary editing in a short time. Everyone assisted in so many ways so *Lazy-Bed Gardening* could be published at this time;

- Mary Campagna and Cynthia Raiser at Ecology Action for proof-reading and editing suggestions; and

- our neighbors, Bill and Joanne Kerrick, for graciously sharing their electricity and their upstairs bedroom for the three weeks it took to do the typesetting.

NOTE ON THE TEXT

We have used **bold text** throughout this book to emphasize the basic principles and concepts of Biointensive gardening as well as the steps to follow in carrying out these principles.

DEDICATION

To the gardeners of the Earth

who are breathing life back into the soil

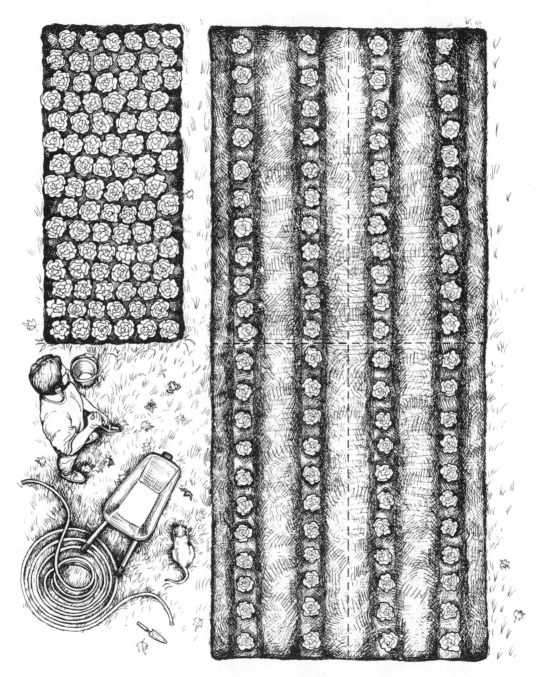

Biointensive fertility—four times the productivity in one-quarter the area!

CHAPTER 1

INTRODUCTION TO LAZY BEDS

Imagine yourself as a plant and think about where you would like to live. You cannot walk around and look for food and shelter -- they have to be within easy reach of your roots. As your roots and root hairs grow out in search of food, they will move more easily through loose, moist soil. You will grow strong and healthy if those roots find an ample supply of microscopic organisms ready and waiting to make nutrients available for your dining pleasure.

The goal of lazy-bed gardening is to **focus on the soil**. It is by creating and maintaining a living, healthy soil that the gardener will be able to grow health-giving food.

WHAT MAKES A LAZY BED LAZY?

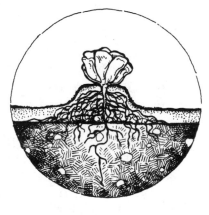

A lazy bed is a *deeply prepared* garden bed whose growing area, *with its closely spaced plants, can produce up to four times more* than an equivalent area prepared less deeply and planted in rows. A lazy bed means less work for the gardener with only one bed to dig, one bed to fertilize, one bed to water, and one bed to weed. And a lazy bed uses only one-quarter the area it would take to produce the same yield by other methods.

Its soil is:

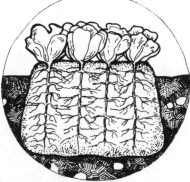

- loosened 2 feet deep,
- evenly moist because water can pass through it easily,
- full of nutrients and organic matter provided by compost,
- and planted with a variety of crops, closely spaced to provide a "living mulch", reflecting nature's diversity.

Because the soil is loosened so deeply, the plant roots are able to penetrate deep into the soil, instead of needing to spread out in search of water and nutrients. For that reason, plants can be spaced more closely in a lazy bed, so that there can be more plants in a lazy bed than in a garden plot using other soil preparation methods. Water is more readily available to plants in a lazy bed because more of it is retained in the deeply loosened soil.

LOOKING BACK TO NATURE

A lazy bed is not a modern invention. Before there were farmers and gardeners, Nature kept the soil covered with a profusion of plants suited to their particular environment. Plants grew best where the soil was the richest, and they did not grow in rows.

Some of the earliest gardeners tried to mimic Nature at her most productive. The Chinese began using biologically intensive, Biointensive, raised beds in food production over 5,000 years ago. The Greeks realized 2,000 years ago that crops grew better in the loose soil of landslides.

Indigenous people in Latin America as early as 2,000 years ago created extensive areas of large raised beds between irrigation channels. In the wet season, they planted their crops on the raised surfaces. During the dry season, when the raised fields were dried out, they planted in the irrigation channels to make use of the water stored within the soil.

In more recent times, the Irish developed their version of raised beds for planting potatoes. They called them *lazy beds* because they knew this method produced more food for their efforts.

Intensive raised-bed systems are not new. They are a proven method for successfully raising large quantities of food, sustainably, over long periods of time.

YOUR LAZY BED

The purpose of this book is to help you start your lazy bed. You will be introduced to a different way of looking at gardening, and you will learn to plan your crops, double-dig your bed, build your compost pile, and raise and transplant your seedlings.

The techniques are simple for getting started in a small, easy to maintain, but highly productive garden which can produce in a very small area all the vegetables -- and more -- for a family of four.

Once you have mastered what this book has to offer, you may find other Ecology Action publications useful:

Jeavons, John. *How to Grow More Vegetables.* 4th ed. Berkeley: Ten Speed Press, 1991.
> The classic book on Biointensive gardening for both beginners and advanced gardeners.

Jeavons, John; Griffin, J. Mogador; and Leler, Robin. *The Backyard Homestead.* Berkeley: Ten Speed Press, 1983.
> For those who want to develop more self-reliance and take their food-raising more seriously.

Duhon, David, and Gebhard, Cindy. *One Circle.* Willits: Ecology Action, 1984.
> Will help you explore your nutritional needs and then design a garden that will produce a complete diet in as little as 700 square feet.

Jeavons, John. *Booklet 14: The Complete 21-Bed Mini-Farm.* Willits: Ecology Action, 1986.

Cox, Carol, and Staff. *Booklet 26: Learning To Grow All Your Own Food.* Willits: Ecology Action, 1991.

A step-by-step approach to sustainably growing all your own food, plus compost crops and a small income in as little as 2,100 square feet.

Donelan, Peter. *Booklet 13: Growing To Seed.* Willits: Ecology Action, 1986.

How to grow all your own seed in the smallest possible area in your own backyard.

CHAPTER 2

THINKING ABOUT GARDENING

You may often hear people say, "I grow my own food." What they usually mean is, "I grow my own vegetables" -- probably summer vegetables, which are only half of their vegetables for all year.

Increasingly, people want to save money and have fresh food to eat. Did you know that you may actually be able to grow **all** of your nutrition in your backyard?

Many gardeners begin by raising tomatoes, cucumbers, onions, green beans and lettuce in a small area. As their garden begins to flourish, potatoes, carrots, corn and melons are often added. Once a garden is successful, other crops like dry beans and grains can be added to these favorite vegetables.

CALORIE CROPS

If you really want to grow your own food, you will need to plant crops that are high in calories, such as beans, dry corn, potatoes and grains.

The U.S. Department of Agriculture[1] now states that we should grow and eat two to four times more grain/cereal and dry bean crops than vegetable crops. These foods, along with fruits and nuts, are ones you can grow abundantly with Biointensive practices right in your own backyard. It is possible to **grow all your food needs easily in a small area** if you are eating

---

[1] USDA Food Pyramid from *EarthSave*, vol. 3, nos. 2-3, Spring & Summer 1992, p. 22.

a vegetarian diet, and as much as 77% of your food needs if you include meat in your diet.

A diet that is nutritionally sound needs to include an adequate amount of calories: the most important nutritional element and the most challenging one to grow in a small area. If we eat enough calories in a varied diet, we are almost certain to be getting enough protein.

One consideration when thinking about gardening is how to grow crops that will provide as many calories as possible in a given area. Dry beans can provide **a lot of calories per pound**, but it takes a lot of space to grow enough dry beans to provide all or most of our calories. Grains are also efficient producers of calories per pound.

We can get a lot more potatoes out of a given area than dry beans, even though a pound of potatoes has less than one fifth the calories that are in a pound of dry pinto beans. A small patch of **potatoes** produces **a lot more calories in a given area** than an equal area of pinto beans.

The chart below helps you compare how many calories you get per pound from each of the calorie crops listed below.

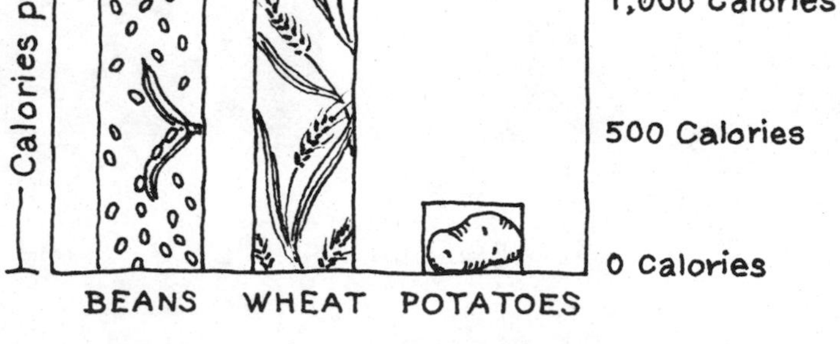

2,000 Calories

1,500 Calories

1,000 Calories

500 Calories

0 Calories

Calories per pound

BEANS   WHEAT   POTATOES

Pinto Beans
        = 1.583 calories

Hard Red Spring Wheat
        = 1,497 calories

Irish Potatoes
        = 297 calories

6

The chart below shows how much space you will need* to grow 1 pound of each of these crops.

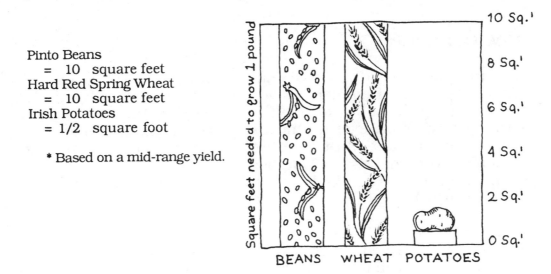

Pinto Beans
   = 10 square feet
Hard Red Spring Wheat
   = 10 square feet
Irish Potatoes
   = 1/2 square foot

* Based on a mid-range yield.

The chart below shows how many square feet are needed to grow 1 person's calorie requirements for 1 year.

Pinto Beans
   = 5,475 square feet
Hard Red Spring Wheat
   = 5,840 square feet
Irish Potatoes
   = 1,570 square feet

Good calorie crops to try are onions and potatoes, as well as dry beans, wheat, oats, rye, and barley. A self-reliant gardener could eventually use up to 90% of the food-raising area for calorie crops and the remaining 10% to grow tasty, fresh vegetables.

COMPOST CROPS

Growing plants need nourishment, just like growing children, and that plant nourishment comes best from a naturally healthy soil. Keeping the soil healthy means making sure it is balanced nutritionally. Whenever we harvest plants from a garden to eat or sell, we are taking nutrients from the soil. Making compost from all garden debris and kitchen waste and putting the compost in our garden beds means that some of the nutrients removed will be returned to the soil.

Composting also happens underground: One Cereal Rye plant can produce 3 miles of root hairs per day, and 387 miles of roots and 6603 miles of root hairs per growing season.

It is important for the soil to have plants growing in it when we are not growing food crops, in order to preserve the health of the soil. When food is not being grown, we can grow plants to use for making compost. Compost provides not only nutrients, but also organic matter, which is good for the soil in many different ways. (See Chapter 5.) Compost crops can also add organic matter directly to the soil in the form of their roots, which are left behind after the plants have been harvested. This is an especially valuable form of organic matter. Gardeners have noticed a difference in the fertility of beds that have had compost crops grown in them and those that have not. **Compost crops "feed" the soil.**

One possible compost crop combination is a mixture of wheat, cereal rye, fava beans and vetch. The extensive roots of the wheat and rye will enrich the soil. The fava beans and grains act as supports, and the vetch sews them all together in a kind of living fabric that is less likely to fall over in wind, rain or snow. Fava beans and vetch also add nitrogen to the soil if they are harvested when about 10% to 50% of their flowers are in bloom. The straw from the wheat and cereal rye provides carbon for the compost pile.

For more on growing compost crops, see Chapter 10.

CHAPTER 3

BEFORE YOU START

The first step in turning your backyard into a productive lazy-bed garden is to think about the beds: their placement, size and arrangement.

SUN AND SHADE

Food and compost crops grow best with **as much sun as possible**. Eleven hours of full sunlight is best, but many plants will grow well with 7 hours. Some plants, like lettuce, can manage with as few as 4 hours of full sunlight, but the best location for garden beds is in the full sun. Remember that the winter sun does not reach as many corners of the garden as the summer sun, and winter compost crops need all the sun they can get.

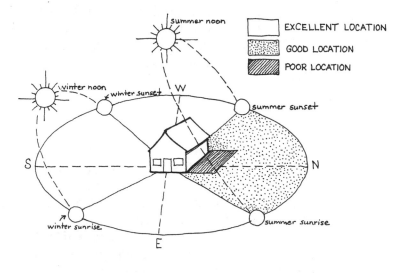

SIZE AND SHAPE OF BEDS

The size and shape of the beds in your garden will depend to some extent on the size of the backyard. They can be circles, ovals, squares, triangles, rectangles or irregular shapes - but there are a few points to keep in mind.

A bed should be at least 3 feet by 3 feet for food production. This size allows the plants to establish a significant mini-climate just **above the soil**, and it allows a significant area for the microorganisms **below the soil surface** to develop. Both of these areas will encourage the healthy growth of the plants.

Since you should not walk on the bed after it has been prepared (unless you use a digging board to distribute your weight so that the soil will not become recompacted), you will need to be able to reach all parts of the bed easily from the path. The width of the bed should allow you to reach the middle of the bed from each side -- up to 5 feet is manageable for most people. The bed can be as long as you want it to be, but you will need to walk around it to get to the other side, so about 20 feet or 25 feet is long enough.

PATHS

If you want your garden to be as productive as possible, you should not waste space on wide paths. The best width for paths is 1 foot. Narrow paths not only make the best use of the garden space, but they also encourage a healthy overall mini-climate in the garden, helping the beds to conserve more water and allowing a "**humidity bubble**" to cover the beds. Some people prefer wider paths for ease in walking and using a wheelbarrow, however.

GARDEN LAYOUT

Laying out several beds in a square garden arrangement rather than in a rectangle helps to conserve moisture and maintain a thriving ecosystem.

A long, narrow arrangement of beds will cause the beds to dry out much more quickly than will a more compact one. When you have decided how to arrange your beds, you can use stakes and string to make sure that the beds and paths are aligned properly.

Once you have decided on a layout it is best to continue to use that plan. As you dig and fertilize your beds year after year, your soil will improve in several ways. Changing the location of beds and paths from year to year would slow down this process.

Some gardeners like to use retaining boards for their beds, but boards are not necessary. They do make a garden look tidy, but they add to the cost of setting up the garden, deplete forests, and may encourage unwelcome insects.

TOOLS

The proper tools will make gardening easier and more productive. Following are the most important tools for the garden:

For **double-digging:**
- a D-handled spade (see below)
- a D-handled fork (see below)
- a digging board (see below)
- a bow rake
- buckets

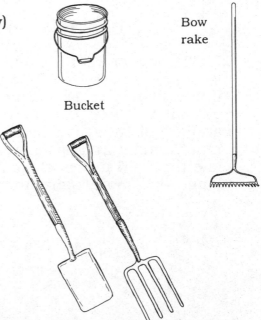

Bucket

Bow rake

D-HANDLED SPADE AND FORK: D-handled tools are easier to dig with. When properly used, they enable you to center your energy and exert the most leverage with the least amount of effort. However, long-handled tools without a D-handle may be better for you if your back is not strong.

11

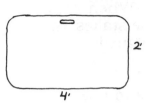

DIGGING BOARD: You can easily make a digging board yourself. It consists of a 5/8- to 7/8-inch-thick piece of exterior plywood, 2 to 3 feet wide and 3 to 5 feet long. A 4-foot by 8-foot piece of plywood can be cut into 4 pieces. You can round the corners, cut out a handle hole to make carrying it easier, and season it with linseed oil.

For **seed propagation:**

- flats (see below)
- a hand fork
- a narrow transplanting trowel
- a widger/kitchen knife/popsicle stick
- labels and a wax pencil or marker
- 1-inch chicken wire screen

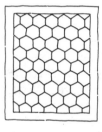

Hand fork

Trowel

Widger
Kitchen knife
Popsicle stick

Labels
Wax pencil

Chicken wire screen

FLATS: If you want to build your own flats, the standard flat size is 3 inches deep by 14 inches wide by 23 inches long. We also find it helpful to have some "half-flats" which are 3 by 14 by 11-1/2 inches. They can be used for smaller numbers of seedlings and are often a good choice because they are lighter. If plants must remain in a flat more than 4 to 6 weeks, they will need one that is 6 inches deep, 14 inches wide and 11-1/5 inches long. (For more information on flats, see Chapter 7.)

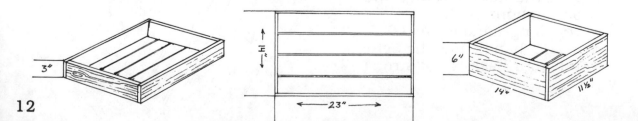

For **watering:**
- hoses
- adjustable hand-grip valve (for varying water pressure easily, as needed, while watering)
- a fan with an on/off valve (used between the hose and the adjustable hand-grip valve, so fans can be changed without going back to the water spigot)
- a Haws-type watering can

Haws-type
watering can

Fan, hose, and
adjustable
hand-grip valve

On/off valve

For **harvesting:**
- small clippers
- sheep shears (especially for grains)
- pruning shears

Small
clippers

Sheep
shears

Pruning
shears

For information on where to buy these tools, see Chapter 13.

14

CHAPTER 4

WHAT DO YOU WANT TO EAT?

CHOOSING WHAT TO GROW

The crops we have suggested for your first lazy bed are vegetables that Americans like to consume fresh and that they enjoy growing in their gardens. The following table shows:

- how much of each vegetable is consumed fresh per person in the U.S. each year,

- how much is produced by commercial U.S. agriculture per 100 square feet,

- how much a 100-square-foot Biointensive lazy bed can produce (depending on the skill level of the gardener),

- how many square feet a beginning Biointensive gardener would need to grow the average U.S. consumption, and, finally,

- how many square feet are suggested for each crop in your first lazy bed.

As your skill and the soil in your lazy bed improve, you will be able to increase your beginning yields to good yields, and then to excellent yields, and **you may choose to reduce the area you need to grow your vegetables.**

	A	B	C	D	E
	U.S. AVERAGE CONSUMPTION PER PERSON lbs/yr., fresh	U.S. AVERAGE YIELD lbs /100 sq.ft.	POSSIBLE BIOINTENSIVE YIELDS Beginning/Good/... .../Excellent lbs/100 sq.ft.	AREA FOR AVERAGE AVERAGE YIELD (sq. ft.)	SUGGESTED INITIAL GARDEN AREA (sq. ft.)

VEGETABLE / SALAD / DESSERT CROPS

Crop	A	B	C	D	E
TOMATOES	17.2	30.7	100-194-418	17.2	10
LETTUCE, LEAF	23.2	48.6	135-202-540	17.2	10
ONIONS, GREEN	D-"4"	D	100-200-540	4.0	2
CORN, SWEET	7.1	15.3	17-34-68 Shelled,Wet	41.7	20
WATERMELON	13.6	24.3	50-100-320	27.2	10
CUCUMBERS	4.0	20.6	158-316-581	2.5	2
SNAP BEANS	1.5	8.2	30-72-108	5.0	2
CARROTS	7.8	58.9	100-150-1,080	7.8	4
CANTALOUPE	7.6	20	50-72-145	15.2	10

CALORIE CROPS

Crop	A	B	C	D	E
POTATOES	52.0	52.6	100-200-780	52.0	25
ONIONS	17.9	68.6	100-200-540	17.9	5
				TOTAL	100
WHEAT (for cereal)	3.1	3.7	SEED: 4-10-26	31.0	25
OATS, Hull-less	3.3	D	SEED: 3-7-13+	47.1	25
DRY BEANS	6.0	2.7	4-10-24	60.0	50
				TOTAL	100

D -- Data not available. For Green Onions, we assume an annual average consumption of 4 lbs.

Column A -- Data from USDA *Agricultural Statistics*, 1987, 1978, and 1972 (except Green Onions).

Column B -- Data from USDA *Agricultural Statistics*, 1972, and other reference sources.

Column C -- Estimates based on our experience and research. Use the lower figure if you are a beginning gardener, the middle figure if you are a good one, and the third figure if you are an excellent one.

Column D -- Column A / Column C (Beginning Biointensive Yield) x 100 = Approximate area needed for a beginning Biointensive gardener to grow the amount given in Column A.

Column E -- Based on getting approximately 1/3 to 2/3 of the average U.S. consumption with beginning Biointensive yields and only one crop in a 4-month growing season. You can also get similar results in a 3-month growing season by using short-season varieties. If you have a 6-month growing season, you may be able to grow more than one crop. See the table that follows.

If your climate is favorable, you will be able to grow more than one crop per season of certain vegetables. The table below indicates the maximum number of crops that may be possible in various growing areas:

CROPS PER GROWING SEASON

	3 mo.	4 mo.	6+ mo.
	(length of growing season)		
Lettuce	1	2	3
Green Onions	1	2	3
Corn	1	1	2
Cucumbers	1	1	2
Carrots	1	2	2

As we discussed in Chapter 2, **calorie crops should be a major part of our diet and should eventually account for 90% of the growing area in our garden,** with **the remaining 10% for vegetable crops.** If the crops in your garden are balanced in this way, the garden may provide **all** of the calories, vitamins, minerals, and other nutrients that you need.

To introduce you to **calorie crops**, we have included **potatoes** and **onions** in your first lazy bed, and we suggest an additional bed, perhaps in your second year, for **wheat** and hull-less **oats** during the cool weather and **dry beans** during the warm weather (see Chapter 12).

YOUR GROWING SEASON

The length of your growing season is determined by when frosts occur in your area. Experienced gardeners plan their garden activities around the first soft frost and the first hard frost in the autumn, and the last hard frost and the last soft frost in the spring. **The time between the last soft frost in the spring and the first soft frost in the autumn is considered to be the optimal growing season for a particular area.** In some areas, the rain determines the growing season. See **My Garden Climate** section on the next page.

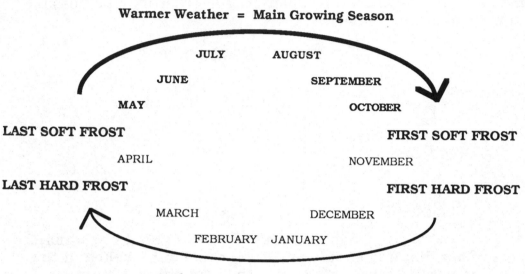

Warmer Weather = Main Growing Season

JULY   AUGUST

JUNE   SEPTEMBER

MAY   OCTOBER

LAST SOFT FROST   **FIRST SOFT FROST**

APRIL   NOVEMBER

LAST HARD FROST   **FIRST HARD FROST**

MARCH   DECEMBER

FEBRUARY   JANUARY

Cooler Weather = Compost Crops

Soft frost: the temperature drops a few degrees below freezing (32°F) for a short time. This may affect more delicate plants.
Hard frost: colder than a soft frost for a longer period. This may kill many plants which are not frost-hardy.

Knowing the length of your growing season is important as you choose seed varieties to grow and as you plan your garden activities.

If you have a **3-month growing season**, it is important to plan carefully and to select seed varieties that will mature in the shortest possible time. Pay particular attention to potato, onion and dry bean varieties.

A **4-month growing season** is a better length for a successful garden. You can choose from a greater number of longer-maturing varieties and expect higher yields with this longer season.

MY GARDEN CLIMATE

Seasonal information:

First SOFT Frost Date:_____ First HARD Frost Date:_____

Last HARD Frost Date:_____ Last SOFT Frost Date:_____

Nighttime low reaches 60°F in the spring:_____

Nighttime low drops below 60°F in the autumn:_____

Number of weeks/months of temperatures over 95°F:_____

Number of weeks/months of temperatures under 28°F:_____

• • **Main Spring Planting Date**

   (1 week after last soft frost):

   _____

• • **Main Growing Period (from spring**

   planting date until first soft frost):

   _____ **to** _____

You can check with your neighbors or your
local agricultural extension agent about the climatic
conditions for your area.

PLANTING DATES
FEB-MAY & AUG-SEPT
MAY-APR & JULY-AUG
APRIL-JULY
MAY-JULY

If you have a **5- or 6-month growing season**, you should use the best (warmest) 3 to 4 months or more of that period for growing your vegetables, for the best results.

If your growing season is **longer than 6 months,** choose the best (warmest) 6 months of that period as you plan your gardening adventure. When you are more experienced, you can look at pp. 158-161 in The Backyard Homestead or check with your local extension agent to learn how to extend your growing season. Experienced neighbors are good sources of advice, as well.

CHOOSING SEED VARIETIES

For people whose food comes from the supermarket, a watermelon is just a watermelon, and a tomato is a (frequently tasteless) tomato. But the backyard gardener who begins to explore the seed catalogs will quickly discover that watermelons can grow in individual-serving sizes and in a variety of color, and can even have wonderful differences in flavor! As for tomatoes, you can choose a Rutgers, a Fireball, a Lincoln or a Mars and so many others. **Choosing a seed variety should take into account:**
- **your growing season:** for a short growing season, choose an early variety;
- **your taste preferences**: yellow, white or red sweet corn, for example;
- **plant characteristic**s: bush or pole beans, for instance; and
- **amount of daylight**: some onions, for example, are adapted to short day-lengths, others to long day-lengths.

It is well worth shopping among several seed catalogs when choosing your varieties. You may find different strains of the same variety that mature earlier or later than others. How quickly a crop matures depends on the climate, and **the maturity time** (or in-ground time) **indicated in seed catalogs**

assumes optimal growing conditions in a climate that is good for the crop involved. In your particular garden climate, a variety may mature earlier, later, or in the same number of days as the catalog indicates.

With vegetable **seeds** widely available in supermarkets and hardware stores, it is easy to take seeds for granted. Yet 92% of all crop varieties in agriculture may be nonexistent by the year 2000, at the current rate of loss of genetic diversity. **One of the best ways to preserve plant diversity is by growing and saving your own seed.** Two easy plants to begin to do this with are lettuce and tomatoes (see the individual crop sections in Chapter 8).

In order to grow and save your own seed, you must **start with open-pollinated seed**, that is, seed produced from flowers pollinated naturally and easily by wind, bees, and other wild insects. The seed companies recommended below offer open-pollinated seed.

Seed Savers Exchange (SSE) (R.R. 3, Box 239, Decorah IA 52101) is doing valuable work in the area of preserving a wide variety of open-pollinated seeds. Their *Garden Seed Inventory*, 3rd ed., contains a wealth of information about more vegetables than you can probably name. Members can exchange seeds.

Bountiful Gardens, a project of Ecology Action, has put together a collection of seeds, to make your work easier at the beginning (see Chapter 13). A Bountiful Gardens seed packet contains enough seeds to sow one 100-square-foot bed, unless otherwise noted. This makes planning easier.

It would be impossible to include every excellent seed company in this book. (A good seed company to support sells only seed with a high germination rate which produces healthy plants with good vigor, and it specializes in, or at least emphasizes, open-pollinated varieties.) The ones we suggest here are to help you in your initial choice of open-pollinated varieties. For a more extensive list of seed companies, see *How To Grow More Vegetables*, pages 153-157.

When you are ready to start choosing your own varieties, here are some possibilities to explore:

TOMATOES: Choose a 3-month variety. Bountiful Gardens' choice is Rutgers (74 days). Garden City Seeds has many open-pollinated, northern-acclimated varieties.

LETTUCE, LEAF:
Bronze Arrow (60 days) -- Bountiful Gardens' choice and our personal favorite: it handles heat well, has a good flavor, grows well spring through autumn
Buttercrunch (50 to 75 days) -- Bountiful Gardens
Simpson (55 days) -- Peaceful Valley -- starts early, tolerates heat well

GREEN ONIONS: Stokes Seeds has a good selection of 60-day varieties (be sure to specify "untreated" seeds).
Ishikura (66 days) -- our personal favorite -- Stokes
White Lisbon (60 days) -- Bountiful Gardens' choice
Long White Summer (60 days) -- Stokes
Southport White Globe (Green Bunching Strain) (65 days) -- Stokes
Hardy White Bunching (70 days) -- Stokes

CORN: Most seed catalogs do not carry a big selection of open-pollinated varieties, but SSE's *Garden Seed Inventory* indicates a wide choice of varieties available from many sources.
Golden Bantam (70 to 83 days) -- Bountiful Gardens' choice
Montana Bantam (65 days) -- Fisher's
Double Standard (73 days) -- Johnny's -- a bicolored (yellow and white) corn (if you want only white corn, plant only white seeds)

WATERMELON: You can choose from five different colors: red, pink, yellow, white or orange!

New Hampshire Midget is your personal-sized watermelon (4 to 6 pounds). (65 to 82 days) -- Vermont Bean Seed

Sugar Baby (6 to 12 pounds) (68 to 86 days) -- Bountiful Gardens' choice

CUCUMBERS:

Straight Nine (66 days) -- Bountiful Gardens' choice

Burpless (55 to 65 days) -- Ledgerwood

Marketmore 86 (63 to 68 days) -- Stokes (specify "untreated" seeds)

Straight Eight (52 to 75 days) -- Abundant Life

Lemon (65 days) -- Peaceful Valley

SNAP BEANS, BUSH:

Derby (57 days) -- a Bountiful Gardens' choice

Blue Lake Oregon Bush (60-day) -- Nichols

Bountiful (42 to 51 days) -- Vermont Bean Seed, Shumway

Baffin (60 days) -- a Bountiful Gardens' choice

Kentucky Wonder Bush (65 days) -- Vermont Bean Seed, Shumway's

Royalty Purple Pod (65 days) -- J. L. Hudson

Roc D'Or (57 days) -- a wax (yellow) bean -- Shepherd's

CARROTS: Burpee's catalog has a diagram showing the shapes and lengths of different carrot varieties.

Danvers varieties (65 to 75 days) -- widely available

Nantes varieties (62 to 70 days) -- widely available

Nantes Tip Top (60 to 70 days) -- Bountiful Gardens' choice

CANTALOUPE: The first two varieties listed below are smooth-skinned and therefore less prone to rotting before harvest, but they are *not* short-season melons (advised for cooler climates).

Haogen (90 to 95 days) -- green -- Bountiful Gardens' choice

Cantalun (90 days) -- orange -- Le Jardin du Gourmet

Far North (70 days) -- salmon, sparse net, early -- Gleckler's

POTATOES: Choose from the 150 **organically** grown varieties described in the Ronniger's catalog. Select a 90-day (or less) variety for a 3-month growing season. The varieties below are some of those listed by Ronniger's as early-maturing (65+ days).

White -- **Anoka**
Yellow -- **Yukon Gold**
Pink -- **Early Rose**
Red -- **Red Norland**
Blue -- **Caribe**

ONIONS: The onions you grow may be either "keepers" that store well or "eaters" that do not. The two varieties below are keepers.

Southport White Globe (65 to 120 days) -- Bountiful Gardens' choice

New York Early (98 days) -- Stokes (be sure to specify "untreated" seeds)

WHEAT: The only sources for a variety of small quantities of grain seeds (enough for 100 to 1,000 square feet per package) are Bountiful Gardens and Johnny's.

Hard Red Spring Wheat -- Bountiful Gardens' choice

HULL-LESS OATS: Available from Bountiful Gardens or KUSA.

DRY BEANS: Available from Bountiful Gardens, Vermont Bean Seed or Johnny's. You can choose among Pinto, Black, Red or White Kidney, and "Tri-Color". Pinto beans have slightly more calories per pound than other dry beans. In short-season areas, you can use the following 85- or 90-day varieties from Vermont Bean Seed Company:

Red Peanut Bean	Red Mexican Bean
Pinto Bean	Swedish Brown Bean
French Horticultural Bean	Yellow Eye Bean
Pink Bean	Jacob's Cattle Bean
Great Northern White Bean	Black Turtle Soup Bean

A short-season variety from Bountiful Gardens is Cranberry Bean (65 days).

SEED COMPANY ADDRESSES

Abundant Life Seed Foundation
    P.O. Box 772   Port Townsend WA 98368
Bountiful Gardens
    18001 Shafer Ranch Road   Willits CA 95490
W. Atlee **Burpee** & Co.
    300 Park Avenue   Warminster PA 18991-0001
Fisher's Garden Store
    P.O. Box 236   Belgrade MT 59714
Garden City Seeds
    1324 Red Crow Road   Victor MT 59875-9713
Gleckler's Seedmen   Metamora OH 43540
J. L. Hudson, Seedsman
    P.O. Box 1058   Redwood City CA 94064
Johnny's Selected Seeds
    Foss Hill Road   Albion ME 04910-9731
KUSA Research Foundation
    P.O. Box 761   Ojai CA 93023
Le Jardin du Gourmet
    P.O. Box 75   St. Johnsbury Ctr. VT 05863
Charles B. **Ledgerwood**
    3862 Carlsbad Blvd.   Carlsbad CA 92008
Nichols Garden Nursery
    1190 N. Pacific Hwy.   Albany OR 97321-4598
Peaceful Valley Farm Supply
    P.O. Box 2209   Grass Valley CA 95945
Ronniger's Seed Potatoes
    Star Route   Moyie Springs ID 83845
Shepherd's Garden Seeds
    30 Irene St.   Torrington CT 06790
R. H. **Shumway's**
    P.O. Box 1   Graniteville SC 29829
Stokes Seeds Inc.
    Box 548   Buffalo NY 14240
Vermont Bean Seed Company
    Garden Lane   Fair Haven VT 05743

CHAPTER 5

PREPARING A LAZY BED:

DOUBLE-DIGGING

The key to a productive, healthy garden is the preparation of the growing beds. **A well-prepared bed with loose soil to a depth of 24 inches allows the roots of the plants to grow evenly and to provide a steady supply of nutrients to the rest of the plant.** Water is able to move through the soil freely, and weeds are easy to pull out. The plant roots have so much loose soil to grow into that more plants can grow in a given area, and this means more food from a smaller garden.

The goal of double-digging is to produce a "**living sponge-cake**" in the soil, to a depth of 24 inches, with 50% pore space for air and water -- optimally half of the pore space for each. (The other 50% of the soil is mineral matter, including rock fragments, and a small amount of organic matter.) In a new garden, the sponge-cake may turn out to be only 15 or 18 inches deep, but the microorganisms, the worms, the plant roots and water

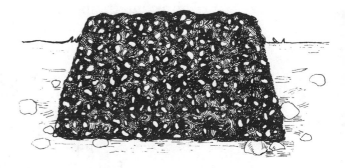

will usually cause it to become a little deeper each year.

Any soil starts with soil particles -- sand, silt and clay in varying proportions -- which constitute its **texture**. The roots (both living and dead) of the plants and the "sticky threads" produced by the soil microorganisms "sew" these particles together to provide a loosened aerated **structure** -- the "living sponge-cake" mentioned above. Once a *good* structure has been established by double-digging, it may be better to use **surface cultivation**, the loosening of the upper two inches of the soil with a cultivating tool, for several years. In this way, the developed structure and soil organic matter are better preserved.   Whenever the lower soil becomes compacted, the bed may be double-dug again to encourage the re-establishment of a well-aerated structure.

The best time to double-dig is in the spring, just when seedlings are ready to be transplanted into the bed. Seedlings grow best in a newly loosened soil. If you are starting a new bed, it is also possible to single-dig (to loosen the soil 12 inches deep with a fork) and sow compost crops (see Chapter 10). Then, in the spring, the double-digging will be that much easier.

STARTING A NEW BED

Before starting a new bed, put in stakes to mark each corner and connect them with string. Depending on the condition of your soil, you may also need to do one or more of the following things in the order indicated:

1. If the soil is dry and hard, water it well (for as much as 2 hours with a sprinkler, if necessary) and let the water seep in for 2 days.
2. Loosen the soil 12 inches deep with a spading fork.
3. Remove any grass and weeds, including their roots. These[1] can go into the compost pile.
4. Water lightly for a day or two (5 minutes or so per 100 square feet), or even longer if the clods are particularly large.
5. Let the soil rest for 1 day.

---

[1] With the exception of crab grass and bermuda grass, which should be thoroughly sun-dried for several months to completely kill them before they are added to the compost pile.

1.

DOUBLE-DIGGING

Stand on a digging board (see Chapter 3) so that your weight is distributed evenly and does not recompact the soil.

1. **Across the narrow end of the bed, dig a trench 1 foot wide and 1 foot deep** with a spade. Put the soil into buckets or a wheelbarrow or pile it on the ground. It can then be put in a bin to use for making compost and flat soil, or it can go back into the bed after the double-digging is completed to fill the last trench. The last trench will not really need this soil because of the increased volume of the aerated soil in the bed, while soil that is used in making compost will be returned to the bed as part of the cured compost.

2.

2. **Loosen the soil in this trench an additional 12 inches with a spading fork**. Dig the fork in to its full depth (or as deeply as possible) and push the handle downward so the fork tines lever through the soil, loosening and aerating it. If the fork will not go through easily, pull it out a little and then push down. You should go only as deep as the tool will loosen easily. The next time you double-dig that bed, you will be able to go a little deeper.

If the soil in the lower trench is dry, water the loosened soil well before continuing. It is easier to get water down into the lower 12 inches of soil at this point than it is after the bed preparation has been completed.

30

3.

3. **Dig out the upper part of the second trench 1 foot deep and 1 foot wide with the spade.** Dig the spade in to its full depth (or as deeply as possible), lift the soil out on the spade pan, tip the spade pan downwards and slide the loosened, aerated soil into the upper part of the first trench. Try to mix the soil layers as little as possible. Different microorganisms live in different soil layers -- the less their living quarters are disturbed when the bed is dug, the more ready they will be to get on with their business of providing nutrients to the newly planted seedlings. Move each spadeful of soil forward in the same way until you have dug across the entire trench.

4. **Loosen the lower 12 inches of soil in the second trench with the fork**.

5. **Continue in this way with the third trench and as many more trenches as you need to finish the bed.**

6. **After the third or fourth trench (and every 3 to 4 trenches after that), rake the accumulated soil forward and level the double-dug portion of the bed.** There will be less soil to move around when you reach the end of the bed and have less energy to move it! (You will not need the soil from the first trench to fill in the last trench, if you are using that soil for compost and flat mix.)

7. **When you have loosened the lower part of the last trench, rake the whole bed level.** (Add the soil from the first trench, if you are not using it for other purposes.)

8. **Spread a 1-inch layer of cured compost over the surface of the bed.**

9. **Sift it into the top 2 inches with a spading fork.**

Rake

Spread

Sift

It is a good idea to put compost on your bed and plant your seedlings as soon as possible after double-digging. If you cannot transplant your seedlings immediately, cover the double-dug bed with a shade net and keep the soil evenly moist to keep the microorganisms alive, Put the compost on the bed just before transplanting.

AVOIDING RECOMPACTION

Once the bed has been dug, try not to walk on it. One of the reasons for double-digging is to put air into the soil. Walking on the bed will recompact the soil. When planting the seedlings in the bed, using a digging board will allow you to distribute your weight over a wider area and minimize compaction.

Compaction destroys the structure of the soil. You have very little control over the **texture** of your soil -- it is either sandy or clayey or something in between. But there are several things you can do to improve the **structure** of your soil -- how your soil holds together. One of them is aerating the soil by double-digging. Another is adding organic matter to the soil in the form of compost (see Chapter 6).

BY HAND?

Some people prefer to let a machine do their digging for them. But your garden soil will not benefit from rototilling. A rototiller destroys the earthworms and other soil creatures that help make your soil fertile. It also compacts the subsoil and destroys the soil's structure. Dr. Robert Parnes, author of *Soil Fertility,* notes that if we are to be sensitive to soil processes, we should avoid rototillers.[2]

---

[2] Robert Parnes, *Fertile Soil: A Growers Guide to Organic & Inorganic Fertilizers.* Davis, CA: agAccess, 1990, p. 6.

HOW LONG SHOULD IT TAKE?

An expert can double-dig an established bed in 1 to 2 hours, but the first time you double-dig, it may take you all day to prepare a 100-square-foot bed, especially if the soil has never been double-dug before.   As you become more familiar with what double-digging is all about, and as your garden gets more used to being double-dug, it will gradually take less and less time and effort to dig a bed.

The important thing is to **take your time** and learn to do it well.   Increased speed will come from experience and skill -- not from rushing, which will only tire you out.

TAKING CARE OF YOUR BACK

When double-digging is properly done, your whole body weight does most of the work, with a little help from your knees and arms. If you feel excessive pressure on your back, you should stop and think about how to put less pressure on it. Use your body weight to push the spade and the fork into the soil.

 **Be sure to place your foot on the spade or the fork so that it is under your arch just in front of your heel.** Your body weight is used more efficiently that way. Lift the spade only as high as you need to and let the soil slide off on its own as you tip the spade. When loosening the soil in the lower trench, use your body weight, rather than your leg and arm muscles, to push the fork through the soil.

If double-digging really seems like it will be too much for you, try to have a friend or neighbor do it for you. You might also consider single-digging and using much wider spacing for the plants.

A DOUBLE-DUG BED = A LAZY BED

When some people hear the term double-digging, they groan: "It's too hard." "It takes too much time." "It's too much work." "It isn't worth it." When other people hear double-digging, they smile. They think of it as **exercise, rather than work.** They know that **a double-dug bed really is a lazy bed, because they can get a good yield in a much smaller area with less digging overall.** They like the fact that double-digging keeps them in touch with the soil in their garden. They know **lazy beds are fun!**

CHAPTER 6

WHAT TO FEED A LAZY BED:

COMPOST

For people who are used to depending on the supermarket for food, it is easy to forget that what we eat depends entirely on fertile soil. Sir Albert Howard, a pioneer of the organic agriculture movement, considered that the fertility of the soil determines the future of civilization.[1] The North African desert, for example, used to be the grain-growing area for Rome -- until it was strip-mined of nutrients by improper farming practices.

Nature manages the fertility of her soil quite effectively with her natural cycles of life and death, growth and decay. Plants and animals live and grow, their leaves, roots and residues enriching the soil of their environment. When they die, moist soil decomposes their bodies and transforms them into organic matter that replenishes the soil and promotes new life and growth. Nature is an expert at **recycling** all of her wastes -- "living" recycling -- so that organic materials, major minerals and trace minerals are continually being returned to the soil to nourish new growth.

THE BENEFITS OF COMPOST

Healthy plants in our gardens need a steady supply of nutrients. They can get 96% of these nutrients from air, water, and the sun (through the process of photosynthesis). If they cannot get the remaining 4%, however, they will not grow well or provide us with healthy food. **Compost**, mixed into the soil, can supply these important **nutrients** if the compost materials have them. Compost improves the **structure** of the soil, making it easier to work, increasing its ability to hold water and air, and reducing

---

[1] Sir Albert Howard, *An Agricultural Testament.* New York: Oxford University Press, 1943, p. 20.

the likelihood of erosion. Seeds grow into seedlings more rapidly in composted soil.

Compost is much better for the soil than chemical fertilizers, which do not add organic matter and some of which can leach out of the soil if the plants do not use them immediately. A compost pile also recycles garden debris, leaves, and kitchen waste into food for the soil.

THE DECOMPOSITION PROCESS

The decomposition process that goes on in the compost pile is carried out by a succession of microscopic organisms, including bacteria and fungi, and larger organisms, including earthworms. Providing the ideal conditions for these organisms is what makes a good compost pile. The compost pile needs:

AIR -- Beneficial bacteria need air to breathe, so compost materials should be piled up loosely, but not too loosely -- too much air is not good, either.

MOISTURE -- Soil organisms need enough water to keep them alive, but not too much -- you do not want to drown them! The pile should be wet, but not too wet -- like a well-wrung-out sponge.

A VARIETY OF MATERIALS -- The greater the variety of materials in a pile, the greater the variety of microbial life, and therefore the higher the quality of the compost and soil. In addition, greater microbial diversity reduces the likelihood of plant diseases.

WARMTH -- Microorganisms are most active during the warmer months of the year when the rate of decomposition is greater. It is important to build compost any time you have materials, however, even when the weather is cooler and decomposition is slower.

As the decomposition process begins, the activity of the microorganisms will cause the pile to heat up. Some microorganisms will die and others will take over, continuing the process. Eventually, the soil organisms will change the original organic materials into a more stable form of organic matter called humus. Humus is a **living fertilizer**, alive with microorganisms consuming other microorganisms that have broken down, recombined and transformed the original organic matter. The nutrients in the humus are easily available to the plants in a slow, natural, continual process. What wonderful gardens there will be when we all develop a better sense of humus!

MATERIALS FOR A COMPOST PILE

The compost pile needs three kinds of materials:

DRY VEGETATION -- dry grass and weeds, leaves, straw, hay, dry compost crops, including some woody materials, such as broken-up corn stalks. Dry material provides carbon that is the energy source for all life forms.

GREEN VEGETATION -- fresh weeds, green grass, kitchen wastes including a small amount of bones (but no meat -- you do not need dogs and raccoons digging through your compost pile -- or large amounts of oil), green compost crops. Green material provides nitrogen that enables the microorganisms to develop their bodies which are necessary to digest their carbon energy source.

DO NOT PUT IN THE COMPOST PILE: cat and dog manure, diseased plants, poisonous plants.

SOIL -- good bed soil with valuable microorganisms to start the decomposition process. The soil will keep down flies and odors, help the pile to hold water, and therefore allow the pile to decompose more slowly, which will ensure an easier-to-maintain compost pile.

Some people like to keep their compost under control in a bin and a few use a drum or an enclosure of some kind. This is not necessary, but if you prefer to use some sort of container, make sure the compost has enough air to breathe, so that the correct kind of decompostion can take place.

BUILDING A COMPOST PILE

When building your pile, think about the layers that make up a dinner casserole -- like lasagna.

1. First, with a spading fork, **loosen the soil** 12 inches deep where you will build your pile. This area should be at least 3 feet square (4 feet or 5 feet would be even better if you have enough space and material), so that the pile will have enough mass to ensure good decomposition. Loosening the soil helps to provide good drainage and aeration. Remember to leave enough space to turn the partially decomposed pile (see 7 below).

2. Put down a 3-inch layer of **rough materials** which can help to aerate the pile: twigs, small branches, corn or sunflower stalks, caneberry or rosebush prunings, and so on.

3. Make your compost "lasagna" **layers**, watering each layer as you go:
   • a 2-inch layer of **dry** materials
   • a 2-inch layer of **green** materials
   • a layer of soil which lightly covers the materials, or about 1/2 of a 5-gallon bucket for a 3-foot by 3-foot compost pile

4. **Continue to add layers** until your pile is about 3 feet high. If your pile is bigger at the base, you can pile the materials 4 feet high or more (but watch that the top of the pile does not start to slide).

You can use a pitchfork to pull out the sides of the pile as you add layers, to keep the pile square.

5. **Cover** the top of the pile with extra soil, to maintain the moisture in the pile. A light layer of straw on top of the soil during the rainy season will keep out excess moisture and will prevent the pile from becoming soggy.

6. **Water** the pile as needed to keep it moist. Check the moisture in the middle of the pile from time to time -- it is easy to either underwater or overwater the pile.

7. **Turn** the pile after about 3 to 6 weeks. The purpose of turning is to bring the drier, less decomposed material on the outside to the inside and the more decomposed material to the outside. A good tool to use is a pitchfork, since it is lighter than a spading fork and is shaped to allow easy turning of the material. Start by loosening the soil in an area about one half to two thirds the original area (since the pile has shrunk), and add a layer of rough materials at the bottom. Move the materials from the original pile to the new pile, bringing the drier materials to the inside. Add water as you go, if necessary, to be sure that the turned pile is evenly moist.

Turned pile   <------   Original pile

8. **Let the pile decompose**, or "cook", for a total of 3 to 6 months. The compost is ready to use when:
- most of the original ingredients are unrecognizable,
- **its smell is fresh and woodsy like fresh spring water**, and
- the material is dark brown or black, soft and crumbly.

9. If you are not ready to use the compost when it is cured, spread it out and let it dry. It is important not to let the pile decompose too long, or the materials will turn into topsoil rather than compost and will lose the high-quality organic matter that has been so carefully built up.

This recipe may make building compost sound more complicated than it is. **The important thing is just to go ahead and build your compost pile as the materials become available, without worrying too much about the details at the beginning.** We recommend this low-maintenance approach, since it is easy and produces such a good result.

The three most important elements in building compost are:

- have **enough air** in the pile,
- **use as many different compost materials as you can**, and
- **keep the compost moist enough**.

As you learn to better understand the composting process and as your garden produces more and more material for you to use, you will be able to improve your technique.

USING YOUR COMPOST

The best time to put compost in your growing beds is in the spring, just before transplanting the seedlings for the major growing season. As a general rule, you can spread 1/2 inch of cured compost over the surface of the bed. This comes to approximately six 5-gallon buckets per 100-square-foot bed.[2] Then work it evenly into the top 2 inches of the soil, using a sifting motion with a spading fork (see Chapter 5). Generally, one application of compost per 4-month growing season is adequate.

COMPOST PILE

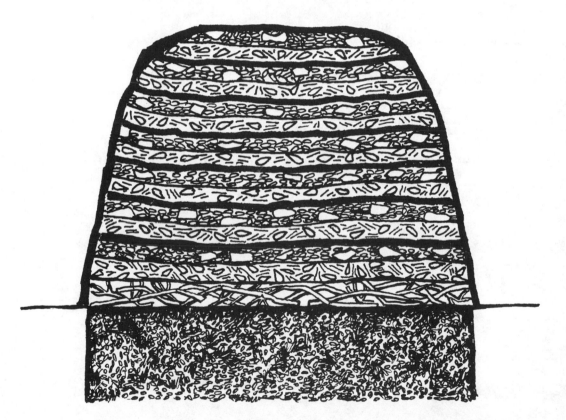

---

[2] Some people prefer to use more soil in their compost, as described in *How To Grow More Vegetables*. If your compost pile has more soil than the one described here, you may cover the bed with 1 inch of cured compost (approximately twelve 5-gallon buckets).

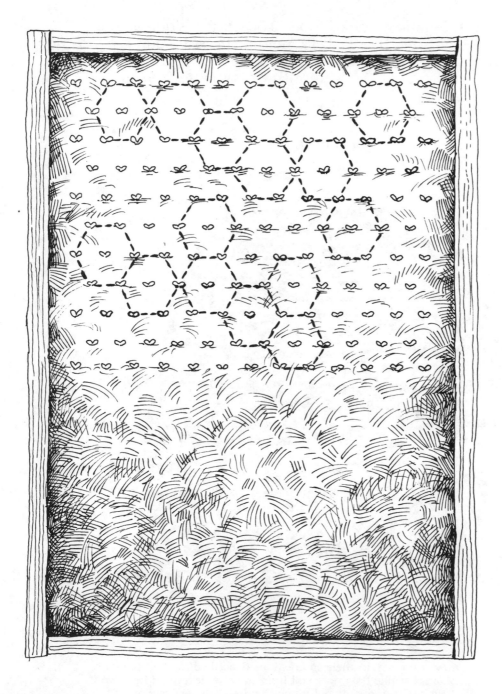

CHAPTER 7

SEEDLINGS

Now that your lazy bed has been prepared and the compost has been spread, you have a choice as to whether to sow seeds directly into the bed or to use seedlings.

Transplanting seedlings involves more advance planning and more time, but in a small garden, it has several advantages:

1. Transplanted seedlings make **better use of bed space**. Seeds can take from 5 days to 12 weeks or more to reach seedling size. If that growing is done in a flat, something else can be growing in the bed in the meantime.

2. You can be reasonably sure that **each transplanted seedling will grow into a healthy mature plant**. Not all seeds germinate, so that, no matter how carefully you plant them, you can end up with gaps between plants and therefore bare soil that allows evaporation.

3. Plants **grow better if they are evenly spaced.** Some seeds are sown by broadcasting, scattering them over the soil. Broadcast seeds -- no matter how evenly you try to scatter them -- will inevitably fall in a random pattern, with some closer and some farther apart than the optimal spacing for best plant growth. The roots of evenly spaced transplanted seedlings can find nutrients and grow more easily, and the leaves of the plants will cover and protect the soil, creating a good mini-climate, so there is better protection for the soil. Carbon dioxide is captured under

the leaf canopy of closely spaced plants. This is where the plants need it for optimal growth. Also, evenly spaced plants best stimulate each other's growth.

4. **Transplanting stimulates growth**. When you transplant a seedling into a double-dug, composted bed that is fluffy, aerated, and full of nutrients, you give it a second "meal" of nutrients, air and moisture after its first "meal" in the flat. Also, if the seeds are sown directly in the bed, while the seeds are germinating and growing into seedlings, the soil will begin to recompact after its initial digging. Because of this, the soil will not be as loose for the plants to grow in once the seedling stage is reached.

5. It takes a lot **less water** for seedlings in a flat (1/2 gallon per day) than for seedlings in a bed (10 to 20+ gallons per day).

FLATS AND FLAT SOIL

Tools for Seed Propagation:
- *1-inch chicken wire screen*
- *widger/ kitchen knife/ popsicle stick*
- *trowel and hand fork*
- *labels*
- *wax pencil or marker*
- *flats*

To raise seedlings, you will need flats and flat soil. Flats should be 3 inches deep to encourage good root growth after germination. The standard 3-inch-deep flat (for use with the Master Charts in this book and *How To Grow More* Vegetables) is 14 inches wide by 23 inches long. A flat this size full of soil and moisture weighs about 40 pounds. A bigger flat will be very heavy and awkward to carry. A half-size flat, 14 inches by 11-1/2 inches, is much easier to carry and especially handy for smaller gardens.

Six-inch-deep flats are good for seedlings that need to stay in the flat more than 4 to 6 weeks to develop deeper roots, such as parsley, tomatoes and members of the cabbage family. Six-inch-deep flats should be 14 inches by 11-1/2 inches, the half-flat size, for lighter weight and easier handling.

A good simple flat soil mix is **one part sifted compost** and **one part bed soil** (saved from the first trench when you double-dig). "Old" flat soil, that has been used to raise seedlings, can be stored in a bin. Although some of the nutrients will have been depleted, it will still be rich in nutrients and organic matter, so it can be used to make new flat mix. In this case, the recipe is one part old flat soil, one part sifted compost and one part bed soil. As your bed soil and your compost improve, your flat soil and seedlings also will improve.

SOWING SEEDS

When you are ready to sow your seeds in the flat, fill the flat with moist (but not too wet) flat soil, making the soil level with the top of the sides and making sure the corners are filled in.

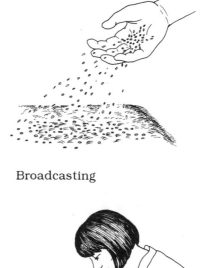

Some seeds are sown by broadcasting, that is, scattering them evenly over the soil surface.

Broadcasting

Others, especially larger seeds, are placed on the soil 1 or 2 inches apart. A piece of 1-inch mesh chicken wire is helpful for keeping the seeds well-spaced. Put a seed in every hole for 1-inch spacing or in every other hole for 2-inch spacing. Cover the seeds with a layer of flat soil which is as deep as the seed is high when it is resting on top of the soil, pat the flat soil down lightly, and water well.

FLAT SEEDING TYPES

Some seedlings can go straight from the flat to the bed. Others that need a longer time in the flat to develop their root systems will need to be "pricked out" into a second and sometimes a third flat.

- **One-time** sowing (**broadcasting**) in a 3-inch-deep flat: onions
- **One-time** sowing on **1-inch centers** in a 3-inch-deep flat: beans, corn, grains (and also beets, spinach, mangels and chard)
- **One-time** sowing on **2-inch centers** in a 3-inch-deep flat: squash, cucumbers, melons
- **Sowing** (**broadcasting**) in a 3-inch-deep flat --> **Pricking-out** on **1-1/2-inch centers** into a 3-inch-deep flat: lettuce
- **Sowing** on **1-inch centers** in a 3-inch-deep flat --> **Pricking-out** on **2-inch centers** into a 6-inch-deep flat: tomatoes (and also peppers, broccoli, cauliflower)
- **Sowing** (**broadcasting**) in a 3-inch-deep flat --> **First pricking-out** on **1-inch centers** into a 3-inch-deep flat --> **Second pricking-out** on **2-inch centers** into a 6-inch-deep flat: (celery and parsley are examples of these)
- **Sowing directly into bed:** carrots (and also radishes)

- **Direct sowing possible, but transplanting preferred:** beans, corn, (and also beets, parsnips, turnips)

PRICKING OUT

Seedlings from broadcast seed are ready to be pricked out **after** their cotyledons (the first "seed leaves" that appear, although they are not the true leaves) have appeared and **before** the roots are too long to handle easily. The second pricking-out should be done when the leaves of the seedlings have just begun to touch each other.

To prick out seedlings, fill a 3-inch- or 6-inch-deep flat with flat soil and mound the soil slightly (remember to fill in the corners). Use a widger (see Chapter 3) or kitchen knife to loosen the soil under the seedlings so that you can lift out one seedling at a time, holding it by its cotyledons and keeping as much soil on the roots as possible.

Then put the widger or kitchen knife into the soil of the second flat at a slight backward angle, just behind where the seedling should be and pull the widger toward you to open up a hole.

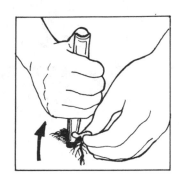

Drop the roots of the seedling into the hole, letting it go a little deeper than it was when it was growing.

Lift the widger out and let the soil fall around the seedling. It is not necessary to spend time carefully pushing the soil up around the seedling; when you water the flat, the soil will settle in around the stem and roots. The seedlings should be arranged on offset, or hexagonal, centers (see page 47) to maximize the space in the flat and **to optimize the mini-climate** that will develop around the seedlings as they grow.

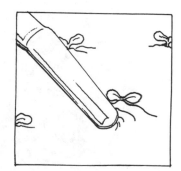

(See Chapter 8 for how to figure out how many flats you need to plant and prick out.)

TRANSPLANTING

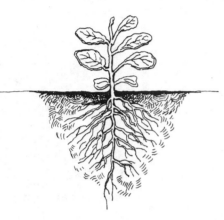

Generally, seedlings are ready to be transplanted into the lazy bed when their leaves are well developed and their roots are forking and vigorous. For most seedlings, root growth should be equal to or greater than leaf growth. Some seedlings, though, will develop roots much faster than leaves. Fava beans ready for transplanting, for example, need to have only a slight amount of green visible - at that point, the root may already be 2 to 3 or more inches long!

As when pricking out, handle the seedlings gently, holding them by the leaves rather than the roots. If you have enough seedlings to choose from, choose the most vigorous and well-developed seedlings to transplant. Use a hand fork to loosen the soil in the flat so that you can lift each seedling out with as much soil as possible.

Open up a hole with a trowel, using the trowel in the same way as the widger (see Chapter 3).

Drop the seedling in, to a depth up to its first true leaves (you can bury the cotyledons). Keep the soil loose (though not too loose); the watering will settle the soil around the roots.

The **best time of day to transplant is in the early evening**. The cooler air makes it easier for seedlings to get established in their new environment.

You may put your digging board on the bed to stand and sit on while you are transplanting. Move the board back as needed, loosening with a hand fork the soil that was just compacted by the digging board.

Water your seedlings every 3 or 4 rows if you are planting a large area, and remember to keep the soil in the seedling flat moist.

If you have any seedlings left over, save them until you are sure that all the ones you have transplanted will survive. If necessary, after a week or two, you can replace any seedlings that have not survived in the bed.

HEXAGONAL SPACING

The best way to plant your flats or beds is to use offset, or hexagonal, spacing. You can get about 10% more plants in a bed if they are planted on hexagonal centers rather than in rows. Each plant variety needs a certain optimal amount of space for its best growth. If plants are arranged in rows using this optimal spacing, there will be unoccupied space that will allow some soil compaction from watering and increased evaporation.

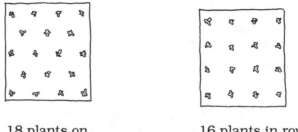

18 plants on
off-set spacing

16 plants in rows
in same area

With offset, or hexagonal, spacing, the leaves of the plants reach out and touch each other on all sides, thus establishing a mini-climate that enhances the plants' growth. This mini-climate is also known as a "**living mulch**". The Greeks believed, and biologists know, that there is the most life where the four elements - Earth, Air, Fire/Heat/Sun, and Water - come together. Thus, the most important part of the plant universe is the area about 2 inches above and 2 inches below the ground around it. If plant leaves can protect all of the soil in a bed, the growing conditions for the plants will be more stable, and both leaves and roots will benefit.

WATERING

Your bed with newly transplanted seedlings needs to have adequate moisture. The best way to water is to create as light a "rain" as possible and to focus on **watering the soil, rather than the plants**. A Haws-type watering can, which sprays the water up into the air, and a watering fan, with an adjustable hand-grip valve attached to a hose, will do the best watering. Water falling on the bed gently will compact the soil less and will not damage the seedlings.

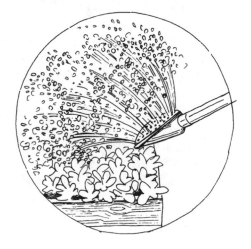

The best time of day to water is in the late afternoon. The garden may also benefit from a midday watering if needed and when that is possible. (In humid climates, be sure to allow enough time after watering for the water to evaporate off of the leaves before the air cools.) How often and how much to water depends on your weather and your soil.

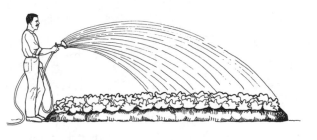

You will gradually learn how much water your particular soil needs at various times of the year. After watering in the evening, check the soil the following morning. Poke your finger into the soil in different parts of the bed. If the soil is evenly moist for the first 2 inches and continues to be moist below this level, you are giving the bed enough water. If the soil is dry or soggy, you need more or less water. The edges of a bed dry out more quickly than the middle, due to more exposure to the sun, air and wind, so give the edges 2 to 3 times more water than the middle of the bed

MINI-GREENHOUSES

A mini-greenhouse made from plastic sheeting and wood can increase the temperature of the soil and the air surrounding the plants and allow the gardener to get an early start on the growing season and to extend the growing season in the autumn. The double-walled construction of the design can keep the inside temperature above the freezing point when the outside temperature falls as low as 20°F. This makes the unit a good season-extender for crops. See *Backyard Homestead* (pages 135-141) for more details and design information.

Mini-greenhouse with the doors flipped open

CHAPTER 8

PLANNING AND PLANTING CROPS

Taking the time to put together a garden plan during the winter months when you are not busy outside will save you a lot of time and make it easy to coordinate the various activities involved in starting your garden in the spring.

YOUR PLANTING DATE

The first step in putting together the plan for your garden is to **establish your main spring planting date.** This is **generally 1 week after the last soft frost.** See **My Garden Climate** in Chapter 4. In Willits, we assume that we will have our last soft frost on May 15, so our main spring planting date is May 21. It is possible to plant cool-weather crops, such as onions, lettuce, potatoes and carrots, earlier than that, but for the purposes of this beginning garden, we will assume that all the crops will be planted at about the same time. If your area does not have frost, you can plant all year, with the hot-weather crops, such as tomatoes, being planted when daytime temperatures reach 80°F and nighttime temperatures are preferably 60°F or higher.

DECIDING HOW MUCH TO GROW

When deciding how much to grow, you may want to figure out about **how much of a particular crop you would like to eat per week**, to keep from growing too much or too little. Here are two examples of how to calculate crop yields, using the Master Chart on pages 58-59:

For 5 heads of lettuce per week:
    • Once lettuce is mature, if it is not too hot, it can be harvested over a 3-week period. So you will need 15 heads of lettuce per crop.
    • On 9-inch centers, up to 248 lettuce plants will fit in one 100-square-foot bed (see Column DD in the Master Chart).
    • Divide 15 heads by 248 heads (to get the percentage of the bed) and multiply by 100 (to convert the percentage to actual square feet). For 15 lettuce plants, you will need at least 6 square feet.

For 2 pounds of snap beans per week:
    • Look at the Weeks Harvest column (Column JJ) for Snap Beans: Snap Beans can be harvested over a 12-week period. Let us assume 10 weeks for planning purposes, since the plants may not be as productive near the end as at the beginning.
    • 2 pounds per week x 10 weeks = 20 pounds. Look at the beginning Biointensive yield in the chart in Chapter 4, Column C. At beginning yields, a 100-square-foot bed will produce 30 pounds of beans.
    • Divide 20 pounds by 30 pounds, then multiply by 100. You will need approximately 67 square feet to grow 20 pounds of beans.

PLANNING

For planning, you will need:
    • the Master Chart in this chapter (or the Master Charts in *How To Grow More Vegetables*, 4th ed., pages 70-98)
    • a current calendar
    • a list of the crops you want to grow and the area you have decided to grow for each one
    • columnar-ruled paper with about 24 columns
    • a calculator
    • a sharp pencil
    • a ruler

On the columnar-ruled paper, identify these columns across the top of the paper (see example, pages 64-65):

CROPS and VARIETY
SQ FT
CENTERS
MAXIMUM NO. OF PLANTS
    PER 100 SQ FT
MAXIMUM NO. OF PLANTS
    ACTUAL AREA
OUNCES SEED
    PER 100 SQ FT
OUNCES SEED
    ACTUAL AREA
NO. OF FLATS TO SOW and CENTERS
NO. OF FLATS TO PRICK OUT and CENTERS
A column for each month
REMARKS   (if there are enough columns)

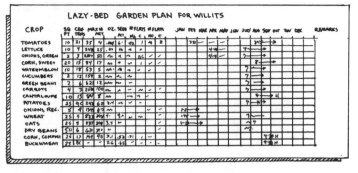

The CROPS column and the REMARKS column need to be wider than the others; the CROPS column should be big enough for the full name of the crop, and the REMARKS column can be used for notes, seed companies, and so on.

THE MASTER CHART

The information you need to plan your lazy-bed garden with the crops we have chosen is contained in the following Master Chart, which is based on the Master Charts in _How To Grow More Vegetables,_ 4th ed., pages 70-98. **The amounts of seed, plants, and so on, are given for a 100-square-foot area and will need to be adjusted for the area you intend to plant.** Once you have decided on the area you would like to use for each crop, you can fill in Column 1 on your garden plan with the square feet. Since all of the amounts in the Master Chart are based on a 100-square-foot bed, you can use the area you have decided on as a percentage of that size of bed. If you want to grow 30 square feet of something, that is 30% of the 100 square feet, and you will multiply the figures in the Master Chart by .30 (that is, 30 / 100).

	AA	BB	CC	DD	EE
	GERM. RATE	OUNCES SEED /100 sq ft	IN-BED SPACING	MAX. PLANTS /100 sq ft	FLAT or BC
VEGETABLE / SALAD / DESSERT CROPS					
TOMATOES	.75	.004	21	35	F
LETTUCE, LEAF	.80	.012	9	248	F
ONIONS, GREEN	.70	.39	3	2,507	F
CORN, SWEET	.75	1.1	15	84	F
WATERMELON	.70	.34	18	53	F
CUCUMBERS	.80	.2	12	159	F
SNAP BEANS	.75	7.8	6	621	F
CARROTS	.55	.2	3	2,507	BC
CANTALOUPE	.75	.09	15	84	F
CALORIE CROPS					
POTATOES	–	23.25-31 lbs.	9"C, 9"D	248	
ONIONS, REGULAR	.70	.21	4	1,343	F
WHEAT (for cereal)	.70	2.4	5	833	F
OATS, Hull-less	.70	3.5	5	833	F
DRY BEANS	.70	12.7	6	621	F
SUMMER COMPOST CROPS					
CORN, SWEET	.75	2.1	12	159	F
BUCKWHEAT	.70	2.6	Broadcast	–	BC
WINTER COMPOST CROPS					
WHEAT (for compost)	.70	2.4	5	833	F
CEREAL RYE	.70	0.9	5	833	F
FAVA BEANS	.70	18.5	21	35	F
VETCH	.70	5.5	Broadcast	–	BC

– MASTER CHART

FF IN-FLAT SPACING	GG PLANTS / FLAT	HH WEEKS IN FLAT	II WEEKS TO MATURITY	JJ WEEKS HARVEST	
VEGETABLE / SALAD / DESSERT CROPS					
1 / 2	187 / 60	4-8 / 3-4	8-13	17+	**TOMATOES**
BC / 1.5	200 / 89	1-2 / 2-3	6-8	–	**LETTUCE, LEAF**
BC (1)	175	6-8	8-17	--	**ONIONS, GREEN**
1	187	2	9-13	--	**CORN, SWEET**
2	42	3-4	10-13	13	**WATERMELON**
2	48	3-4	7-10	26	**CUCUMBERS**
1	187	1-2	8	12	**SNAP BEANS**
–	--	–	9-11	--	**CARROTS**
2	45	3-4	12-17	13	**CANTALOUPE**
CALORIE CROPS					
See text for instructions.			17	–	**POTATOES**
BC (1)	175	12-14	14-17	–	**ONIONS, REGULAR**
1	175	1-2	16-18	–	**WHEAT (for cereal)**
1	175	1-2	13-17	–	**OATS, Hull-less**
1	175	1-2	12	8	**DRY BEANS**
SUMMER COMPOST CROPS					
1	187	2	9-13	--	**CORN, SWEET**
–	--	–	9-13	--	**BUCKWHEAT**
WINTER COMPOST CROPS					
1	175	1-2	16-18	–	**WHEAT (for compost)**
1	175	1-2	16-18	–	**CEREAL RYE**
1	175	1-2	17-26	–	**FAVA BEANS**
–	--	–		–	**VETCH**

NOTES ON MASTER CHART ON PAGES 58-59

Column AA -- Minimum legal germination rate.

Column BB -- Adjusted for the germination rate, offset spacing, and curved surface. May be less for corn, watermelon and oats, depending on seed size.

Column CC -- In-bed spacing in inches.

Column DD -- Maximum number of plants that will fit in a 100-square-foot bed with the in-bed spacing indicated in Column CC. This takes into account the curved surface of the double-dug bed and the offset spacing. This is a maximum -- if your soil structure does not produce a curved surface after double-digging, fewer plants will fit in your bed.

Column EE -- Sow seeds in flats (**F**) or broadcast seeds directly into the bed (**BC**).

Column FF -- Left-hand number is for initial seeding in flat. Right-hand number is for later pricked-out spacing in another flat, when that is recommended. For **lettuce**, the pricked-out flat should be 3 inches deep. For **tomatoes** and most **other crops** that will be pricked out, the second flat should be 6 inches deep.

Column GG -- See note for Column FF. See Chapters 3 and 7 for standard flat size. Approximately **250** seeds/plants will fit on **1**-inch centers; approximately **60** will fit in a standard flat on **2**-inch centers.

Column HH -- See note for Column FF. The range of weeks given depends on the temperature -- in warmer climates, use the shorter time; in cooler climates, use the longer time. Experience will eventually be your guide.

Column II -- Approximate number of weeks to maturity after transplanting.

Column JJ -- Harvesting period in weeks, depending on variety and weather.

ADJUSTING THE FIGURES IN THE MASTER CHART FOR YOUR GARDEN

A simple equation will allow you to figure out how much to grow in your own garden. For example, if you are growing a 100-square-foot bed of corn, you will need 84 plants (Col. DD). If you want to grow only 20 square feet of corn, multiply 84 by .20. You will need a maximum of 16.8 (or 17) corn seedlings to transplant. **You will need to sow more** than 17 **seeds in the flat**, however, **because they may not all germinate**.
So you divide 17 by the germination rate for corn in Column AA of the Master Chart (17 ÷ .75 = 22.67) to find out that you need to sow 23 seeds in order to be sure to have 17 seedlings ready to transplant.

HOW MANY FLATS TO SOW

There are two ways **to figure out** how many flats are needed. **Use the number of living plants you need for your area** (Column 4 on your garden plan). Look at Columns FF and GG in the Master Chart.
Generally speaking, seeds are sown on 1-inch centers in a 3-inch-deep flat, then pricked out, if necessary (depending on the time they need to spend in the flat and the size they need to reach before being transplanted), on 2-inch centers in a 6-inch-deep flat (see Chapter 7). For the initial sowing, divide the number of plants you need by the (lefthand) number in Column GG (which has already been adjusted for the germination rate). This will tell you what proportion of a standard flat you need to sow.

Another way to do the same calculation is to divide the number of plants you need by the germination rate; this tells you that you need to plant so many seeds in order to ensure that you have enough living plants to transplant into the bed. Column GG indicates that a standard flat can hold 250 seeds on 1-inch centers, so you divide the number of seeds you need to plant by this maximum of seeds per flat to find the proportion of the flat that must be planted.

THE DATE COLUMNS

• For the date columns, **you will need to work backwards, starting with your last soft frost date** (May 15 for Willits). **Approximately 1 week later you can transplant** (TP) **your crop into the garden beds** (5/21 TP).

• Now, look at Column HH to see **how long the plants are in the flat before they are transplanted. Count backwards from the transplanting date, and this will give you the date to sow your seeds in flats** (that is, 4/21 F). While you are still learning, it is best to use the higher number of weeks the seedlings are in the flat if there is a range.

• **To find out** the maturity date, or **the time to harvest** (H), **see Column II, and count, from the day you transplant your crop, the weeks it will take the crop to mature.** This will tell you when you can expect to start harvesting your crop.

• **The last dates scheduled are when to sow autumn-winter compost crops.** Most compost crops should be in the bed **before the first rain and/or soft frost, about 1 month before your first hard frost** (Willits, October 15; your area, _____).

PUTTING TOGETHER YOUR PLAN

Go through the **crop information descriptions below so you will understand how to use the Master Chart to put together your garden plan.** Refer to the **Sample Lazy-Bed Garden Plan** put together for the Willits area. You will need to **adjust the dates to correspond to the climate in your area** (see **My Garden Climate** in Chapter 4). The **advantage of** taking the time to do **a garden plan** during the winter months is that you will have **all of the information you need** about your garden activities

together **in one place,** organized and **ready to use** when you
need it.

SAMPLE LAZY-BED GARDEN PLAN

On the two following pages, you will find a sample garden plan
written out for the Willits lazy bed. On the two pages after that
is a blank garden plan for you to photocopy and use for planning
your own lazy bed.

Codes Used For Garden Plan

BC = Broadcast
F = Flat (sow seeds in the flat)
PO = Prick out (into a second flat)
TP = Transplant (into the bed)
H = Harvest

Additional information necessary for the use of the Master Chart
continues after the garden plans.

CROP – Variety	① SQ. FT.	② CEN-TERS	MAXIMUM NUMBER OF PLANTS ③ /100	④ Actual	OUNCES SEED NEEDED ⑤ /100	⑥ Actual	NUMBER OF FLATS TO SOW ⑦ No.	⑧ Centers	NUMBER OF FLATS TO P.O. ⑨ No.	⑩ Centers
TOMATOES – Rutgers	10	21	35	4	.004	6 seeds .0004	.02	1	.06	2
LETTUCE – Bronze Arrow	10	9	248	25	.012	32 seeds .0012		BC	.25	1.5
ONIONS, GREEN – Ishikura	2	3	2,507	50	.39	.0078	.28	BC	—	—
CORN, SWEET – Montana Bantam	20	15	84	17	1.1	23 seeds .22	.09	1	—	—
WATERMELON – Sugar Baby	10	18	53	5	.34	8 seeds .034	.11	2	—	—
CUCUMBERS – Marketmore 86	2	12	159	2	.2	4 seeds .004	.06	2	—	—
SNAP BEANS, BUSH – Roc D'Or	2	6	621	12	7.8	16 seeds .156	.06	1	—	—
CARROTS – Nantes TipTop	4	3	2,507	100	.2	.008	—	—	—	—
CANTALOUPE – Cantalun	10	15	84	8	.09	11 seeds .009	.17	2	—	—
POTATOES – Red Norland	25	9"c, 9" deep	248	62	23.25– 31 lbs.	5.8– 7.75 lbs	—	—	—	—
ONIONS, REGULAR – New York Early	5	4	1,343	67	.21	.01	.38	BC	—	—
WHEAT – Hard Red Spring	25	5	833	208	2.4	.6	1.18	1	—	—
OATS – Hull-less	25	5	833	208	3.5	.87	1.18	1	—	—
DRY BEANS – Black Turtle	50	6	621	310	12.7	6.35	1.77	1	—	—
CORN FOR COMPOST – Montana Bantam	25	12	159	40	2.1	.52	.21	1	—	—
BUCKWHEAT	25	BC	—	—	2.6	.65	—	—	—	—

64 SAMPLE LAZY-BED GARDEN PLAN FOR WILLITS

JAN.	FEB.	MAR.	APR.	MAY	JUN	JUL.	AUG.	SEP.	OCT.	NOV.	DEC.
	2/21 – 4/1 F	3/21 – 5/1 PO		5/21 TP			8/15 H →				
			4/14–5/1 F 4/21–5/7 PO	5/21 TP		7/21 H →					
		3/21–4/7 F		5/21 TP		7/21 H →					
				5/7 5/21 TP							
			4/21–28 F	5/21 TP		7/26 H →			10/1 BC		
			4/21–28 F	5/21 TP		7/21 H →			Compost Crops		
				5/8–15 F 5/21 TP		7/21 H →					
				5/21 BC		7/21 H →					
			4/21–28 F	5/21 TP			8/21 H →				
		ORDER	4/21 Sprout	5/21 TP		7/26 H					
1/7–21 F				5/21 TP			8/30 H				
1/15–21 F	2/1 TP					~7/15 H					
1/15–21 F	2/1 TP					~7/15 H			10/1		
				5/7–14 F 5/21 TP			8/21 H		BC		
						~7/1 F ~7/15 TP		9/30 H		Compost	
						~7/15 BC		9/30 H		Crops	

BC = Broadcast   F = Flat   H = Harvest   PO = Prick Out   TP = Transplant

65

CROP — Variety	① SQ. FT.	② CEN- TERS	③ MAXIMUM NUMBER OF PLANTS /100	④ Actual	⑤ OUNCES SEED NEEDED /100	⑥ Actual	⑦ NUMBER OF FLATS TO SOW No.	⑧ Centers	⑨ NUMBER OF FLATS TO P.O. No.	⑩ Centers

GARDEN PLAN

JAN.	FEB.	MAR.	APR.	MAY	JUN.	JUL.	AUG.	SEP.	OCT.	NOV.	DEC.

BC = Broadcast   F = Flat   H = Harvest   PO = Prick Out   TP = Transplant

The following paragraphs describe how to use the Master Chart to figure out the amounts you need for your garden. If you simply want to know what steps to follow, you can read only the instructions **in bold**.

TOMATOES (10 square feet):

<u>**Growing Instructions:**</u> **Use** .004 ounce (1/8 level tsp) of seed per 100 square feet (Col. BB) or .0004 oz (see below) for 10 square feet (.004 ounce x 10 sq ft/100 = .0004). On 21-inch centers, a 100-square-foot bed will hold up to 35 plants, so a 10-square-foot area will hold a maximum of 4 plants (35 plants x 10 sq ft/100 = 3.5). To ensure 4 tomato seedlings to transplant, you will need to **sow 6 tomato seeds** (4 ÷ .75 germination rate [Col. AA] = 5.3). 6 seeds on 1-inch centers (Col. FF upper) will take up **approximately 2/100 of a standard flat** (6 ÷ 250 [see note for Col. GG] = .024). Or you can use the left-hand number in Column GG which is already adjusted for the germination rate: 6 ÷ 187 = .032. Therefore, sow the seed **on 1-inch centers** (Col. FF left) in 2/100 to 3/100 of a flat (Col. EE) 7 to 12 weeks (total of weeks in Col. HH) before the expected planting date (Willits, February 21 to April 1; your area, _____) and **leave the flat in a warm area.** After 4 to 8 weeks (Col. HH upper), when the **seedlings are 2 to 3 inches tall, prick them out on 2-inch centers** (Col. FF right) in a 6-inch-deep flat. You will need to use 1/10 of a full-sized 6-inch-deep flat (6 ÷ 60 [Col. GG right] = .1) or **2/10 of a** flat if you use the **half-sized 6-inch-deep flat. Transplant** the seedlings into the bed on 21-inch centers (Col. CC) about 1 week after the last soft frost (Willits, May 21; your area, _____), **when the seedlings are about 5 to 6 inches tall. Put a 7- to 8-foot stake beside each seedling** (making sure **at least 1 foot of the stake is in the ground**) and, **as the plant grows, tie the branches loosely (using a figure-8 loop) to the stake.** Let the plant grow as it likes -- **it is not necessary to pinch off any shoots.**

Harvest when the tomatoes are full and ripe. Keep the ripe ones picked to encourage further fruiting.

Saving for Seed: To save seed from tomatoes grown from open-pollinated seed, squeeze the tomato seeds and pulp out of ripe tomatoes from several plants into a jar and add a little water. Leave them in the jar, uncovered, for about 4 days, until they begin to ferment -- you will see a white mold form on the surface of the water. Pour the seeds and pulp into a strainer and wash with clean water. Put the seeds on a paper towel to dry. Store in a cool, dry place.

LETTUCE (10 square feet): If the temperature is over 80°F, it is important to freeze the lettuce seed in a jar for 4 days before planting it, to help trigger germination.

Lettuce is a cool-weather crop, so it will appreciate being shaded by another crop, such as corn or tomatoes, or having a 30%-density shade net over it once the temperature goes higher than 70° to 85°F. Taking the shade net off after the heat of the day and putting it back on in the morning before the heat of the day will help the lettuce to grow faster. Also, lettuce likes midday watering in summer to keep it cool.

Growing Instructions: Use .012 ounce (1/4 tsp) of seed per 100 square feet (Col. BB) or .0012 ounce **(1/32 tsp) for 10 square feet** (.012 oz x 10 sq ft/100). On 9-inch centers (Col. CC), a 100-square-foot bed will hold up to 248 plants, so a 10-square-foot area will hold a maximum of 25 plants (248 plants x 10 sq ft/100 = 24.8). To ensure 248 lettuce seedlings to transplant, you will need to sow 330 lettuce seeds. But since you will broadcast the seeds (rather than sowing them on 1-inch centers), and since you actually need 248 plants, 1 flat will be enough (see note for Col. GG). **Broadcast** (Col. FF left)

the seeds in one flat for 100 square feet or **1/10 of a flat for 10 square feet**, 3 to 5 weeks (total of Col. HH) before the scheduled planting date (Willits, April 14 to May 1; your area, _____). **When the cotyledons are developed, prick out the seedlings on 1-1/2-inch centers** (Col. FF lower) into 2-3/4 3-inch-deep flats for 100 square feet (248 ÷ 89 [Col. GG lower] = 2.78) or **approximately 1/4 of a 3-inch-deep flat** (2.75 x 10 sq ft/100 = .275) **for 10 square feet. When the seedlings are about 2-1/2 to 3 inches tall and have strong, forking roots, transplant** them into the bed on **9-inch centers** (Col. CC). Germination and growth will take longer in cool weather.

Lettuce has best flavor if harvested before sun-up.

Harvest a mature head by cutting it off at ground level, or leave the plants in the ground and harvest only the outside leaves.

<u>**Saving for Seed:**</u> Let one or two lettuce plants continue to grow until flowers appear at the top of the long stalks. When a

significant proportion of the flowers has turned to "fuzz", pull the plant out by the roots and hang it upside down to dry, with the seed heads in a brown paper bag or other suitable bag to allow the seed heads to dry. When the seed heads are thoroughly dry, rub them between your hands to separate the seeds from the chaff. Store the seeds in a cool, dry place.

GREEN ONIONS (2 square feet): Green onions may be kept in the bed until you are ready to eat them. <u>**Growing Instructions: Use**</u> .39 ounce of seed (1 tablespoon + 1-1/4 tsp) per 100 square feet (Col. BB) or .0078 ounce **(1/8 tsp) for 2 square feet** (.39 oz x 2 sq ft/100 = .0078). **Broadcast** (Col. FF) **the seeds** into 6 flats for 100 square feet or **12/100 of a flat for 2 square feet** (about 6 seeds per square inch), 6 to 8 weeks (Col. HH) before the scheduled planting date (Willits, March 21 to April 7; your area, _____). **Transplant on 3-inch centers** (Col. CC) **when the seedlings are about the thickness of ordinary pencil lead.** Have patience and remember to stand and stretch while transplanting! (You might consider planting part of the bed each day.)

Harvest after 2 months (Col. II) or when the plants are the thickness of your little finger to your index finger.

CORN (20 square feet):
<u>**Growing Instructions:**</u> **Use** approximately 1.1 ounces (scant 1/4 cup) of seed per 100 square feet (Col. BB) or .22 ounce **(2/3 tablespoon) for 20 square feet** (1.1 ounces x 20 sq ft/100 = .22). On 15-inch centers (Col. CC), a 100-square-foot bed will hold up to 84 plants, so a 20-square-foot area will hold a maximum of 17 plants (84 plants x 20 sq ft/100 = 16.8). To ensure 17 corn seedlings to transplant, you will need to sow **23 corn seeds** (17 ÷ .75 germination rate [Col. AA] = 22.6). 23 seeds on 1-inch centers (Col. FF) will take up approximately 1/10 of a standard flat (23 ÷ 250 [see note for Col. GG) = .09). (Or you can use Col. GG which is already adjusted for the germination rate: 17 ÷ 187 = .09.)
Therefore, 2 weeks (Col. HH) before the expected planting date (Willits, May 7; your area, _____), **sow the seed on 1-inch centers** in **1/10 of a flat** (Col. EE). **When the seedlings are about 1 inch tall, transplant** them into the bed on **15-inch centers** (Col. CC), taking care to keep the root as vertical as possible.

Harvest the corn when the juices in the seeds are halfway between clear and milky. You can check this by puncturing a few seeds with the edge of your fingernail.

WATERMELON (10 square feet):
<u>**Growing Instructions:**</u> **Use** .34 ounce (1-1/2 tablespoons) of seed per 100 square feet (Col. BB) or .03 ounce **(1/4 tsp) for 10 square feet** (.34 oz x 10 sq ft/100

= .034). On 18-inch centers (Col. CC), a 100-square-foot bed will hold up to 53 plants, so a 10-square-foot area will hold a maximum of 5 plants (53 plants x 10 sq ft/100 = 5.3). To ensure 5 watermelon seedlings to transplant, you will need to sow **7 watermelon seeds** (5 ÷ .70 germination rate [Col. AA] = 7.1). 7 seeds on 2-inch centers (Col. FF) will take up a little more than 1/10 of a standard flat (7 ÷ 60 [see note for Col. GG] = .11). (Or you can use Col. GG which is already adjusted for the germination rate: 5 ÷ 42 = .11.) Therefore, 3 to 4 weeks (Col. HH) before the expected planting date (Willits, April 21 to 28; your area, _____), **sow the seed** on **2-inch centers** (Col. FF) in **approximately 1/10 of a flat** (Col. EE). **When the seedlings have 2 to 3 true leaves** (in addition to the cotyledons, or seed leaves), **transplant** them into the bed on **18-inch centers** (Col. CC), **setting the plants in up to the cotyledons.**

Harvest when the watermelon says "PLUNK!" when you tap it with a knuckle. If it says "Plink!" or "Plank!", it is not yet mature enough.

CUCUMBERS (2 square feet):

<u>Growing Instructions:</u> **Use** .2 ounce (2 tsp) of seed per 100 square feet (Col. BB) or .004 ounce (see below) for 2 square feet. In fact, you will need only 2 plants for 2 square feet since the plants are on 12-inch centers (Col. CC), so you should sow **3 seeds** (2 plants ÷ .80 germination rate = 2.5). 3 seeds on 2-inch centers (Col. FF) will take up a little more than 5/100 of a standard flat (3 ÷ 60 [see note for Col. GG] = .05). (Or you can use Col. GG which is already adjusted for the germination rate: 2 ÷ 42 = .047.) **Sow** the seed on **2-inch centers** (Col. FF) **in 5/100 of a flat** (Col. EE) 3 to 4 weeks (Col. HH) before the expected planting date (Willits, April 21 to 28; your area, _____). Keep the flat in a warm place. **When the seedlings have 2 to 3 true leaves, transplant them into the bed on 12-inch centers** (Col. CC), **setting the plants in up to the cotyledons (seed leaves).**

Harvest when the fruits are swollen, smooth, and green, and before they begin to turn yellow.

SNAP BEANS (2 square feet):
Growing Instructions: Use 7.8 ounces (1-1/4 cup) of seed per 100 square feet (Col. BB) or .15 ounce **(1 slightly rounded tsp) for 2 square feet** (7.8 oz x 2 sq ft/100 = .156). On 6-inch centers (Col. CC), a 100-square-foot bed will hold up to 621 plants, so a 2-square-foot area will hold a maximum of 12 plants (621 plants x 2 sq ft/100 = 12.4). To ensure 12 snap bean seedlings to transplant, you will need to sow **16 snap bean seeds** (12 ÷ .75 germination rate [Col. AA] = 16). 16 seeds on 1-inch centers (Col. FF) will take up less than 1/10 of a standard flat (16 ÷ 250 [see note for Col. GG] = .06). (Or you can use Col. GG which is already adjusted for the germination rate: 12 ÷ 187 = .06.) Therefore, 1 to 2 weeks (Col. HH) before the expected planting date (Willits, May 8 to 15; your area, _____), **sow the seed** on **1-inch centers** (Col. FF) **in approximately 1/10 of a flat** (Col. EE). **When the seedlings have 2 to 3 true leaves** (in addition to the cotyledons, or seed leaves), **transplant them into the bed** on **6-inch centers** (Col. CC), setting the plants in up to the cotyledons.

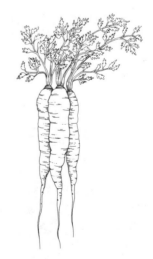

Harvest when the pods are bulging with seeds.

CARROTS (4 square feet):
Growing Instructions: Use .2 ounces of seed (3-1/2 tsp) per 100 square feet (Col. BB) or .008 ounce **(1/8 tsp) for 4 square feet** (.2 oz x 4 sq ft/100 = .008). **Broadcast (scatter) the seed** (Col. BB) **directly into 4 square feet of the bed** (Col. EE) on your planting date (Willits, May 21; your area, _____). The amount of seed has been adjusted for the low (55%) germination rate for carrots (Col. AA). Broadcasting the seed perfectly would result in 2 seeds per center on 3-inch centers (Col. CC), with, on average, only 1 seed per center germinating. Chop the seed in lightly with a rake, using an up-and-down motion.

Harvest after the carrots have been growing for 60, 75, or 90 days, according to the variety and your personal preference.

CANTALOUPE (10 square feet):

Growing Instructions: Use .09 ounce (1/2 tablespoon) of seed per 100 square feet (Col. BB) or .009 ounce **(1/2 tsp) for 10 square feet** (.09 oz x 10 sq ft/100 = .009). On 15-inch centers (Col. CC), a 100-square-foot bed will hold up to 84 plants, so a 10-square-foot area will hold a maximum of 8 plants (84 plants x 10 sq ft/100 = 8.4). To ensure 8 cantaloupe seedlings to transplant, you will need to sow **11 cantaloupe seeds** (8 ÷ .75 germination rate [Col. AA] = 10.6). 11 seeds on 2-inch centers (Col. FF) will take up a little less than 2/10 of a standard flat (11 ÷ 60 [see note for Col. GG] = .18). (Or you can use Col. GG which is already adjusted for the germination rate: 8 ÷ 45 = .17). Therefore, 3 to 4 weeks (Col. HH) before the expected planting date (Willits, April 21 to 28; your area, _____), **sow** the seed on **2-inch centers** (Col. FF) in **approximately 2/10 of a flat** (Col. EE). **When the seedlings have 2 to 3 true leaves** (in addition to the cotyledons, or seed leaves), **transplant** them into the bed on **15-inch centers** (Col. CC), **setting the plants in up to the cotyledons.**

Harvest when the outer skin begins to change color and when the portion around the vine, which attaches the melon to the plant, begins to soften.

POTATOES (25 square feet):

Growing Instructions: Potatoes for planting (23-1/4 to 31 lbs for 100 square feet [Col. BB]; **5-8/10 to 7-3/4 pounds for 25 square feet** [23-1/4 lbs x 25 sq ft/100 = 5-8/10]) should be **ordered to arrive at least 1 month before the scheduled planting date.** Put them to **sprout in a warm place with 50% to**

60% humidity (if they are at 90% humidity for 24 hours with the temperature at 70°F, they can get blight). To sprout potatoes, place them, 1 month before planting (Willits, April 21; your area, _____), in a **warm, lighted area.** Sprouts should **not** grow **any longer than 3 inches**.

There **should be 2 to 3 "eyes" for each large-egg-sized potato**, or, if the potato is very large, it should be cut up into several pieces and set out to dry for 2 to 3 days in a warm, dry, dark place.

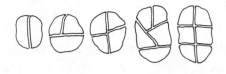

Plant sprouted potatoes or potato pieces 9 inches deep on 9-inch centers (Col. CC), **in 25 square feet of your double-dug bed.**

OUR POTATO-PLANTING TECHNIQUE

After the lower trench has been loosened, Irish potatoes may be placed on its surface on 9-inch centers using offset, or hexagonal, spacing (see Chapter 7). The soil from the next trench's upper level may then be moved forward onto them. -- Mark the location of the potatoes with stones or sticks in the outside paths before covering the potatoes with soil. This will indicate where potatoes should be placed on the surface of each succeeding lower trench. -- This is the easiest way we have found to plant potatoes.

STAKING POTATOES FOR BETTER GROWTH

Potatoes like cool weather. In many warmer areas, we have gotten higher yields by staking up the potatoes as described below. This enables the potato vines to stand up straight and create a better mini-climate, which keeps the plants and soil cooler.

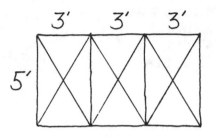

3' 3' 3'

5'

Put 5-foot stakes (1 inch by 1 inch) 1 foot deep in the soil at the corners of the potato section and at 2-1/2- to 3-foot intervals. Tie string to the stakes, 1 foot from the ground and at 1-foot vertical intervals, around the outside of the bed and also crisscrossing the bed, to support the plants.

Be sure to water well. Most of the potato tuber develops in the last 30 to 45 days of its growing period, so be careful not to harvest early.

Harvest any time after flowering, preferably after approximately 90% of the green matter has died back. Use a fork to dig carefully, starting from the side of the bed. Store the potatoes in a dark, humid, cool location; if they are stored in the light, they will turn green and will not be edible.

ONIONS, REGULAR (5 square feet):

Growing Instructions: **Use** .21 ounce (1 tablespoon) of seed per 100 square feet (Col. BB) or .01 ounce **(1/4 tsp) for 5 square feet** (.21 oz x 5 sq ft/100 = .01). **Broadcast** (Col. FF) the seeds into 8 flats for 100 square feet or **1/2 flat for 5 square feet** (about 6 seeds per square inch) 12 to 14 weeks (Col. HH) before the scheduled planting date (Willits, January 7 to 21; your area, _____). **Transplant** on **4-inch centers** (Col. CC) on the scheduled planting date (Willits, May 21; your area, _____), **when seedlings are preferably the thickness of ordinary pencil lead.**

Harvest: When the first onion tops begin to dry and fall over, bend down all of the tops. About 1 week later, stop watering and let the onions stay in the ground for another week or so to cure. Then, using a digging fork or a smaller border fork, start at one end or one side of the bed, loosen the soil under the onions and lift them out. Spread them to dry in a shady, aerated place. Leave the dry tops on and store in a mesh bag, or braid several onion tops together to make an onion braid.

You can cut out the root section of an onion and plant it – you will get another onion!!

(See Chapter 12 for wheat, oats and dry beans.)

THE GARDEN MAP

Once you have determined the area you want to grow for each crop, you can **decide about the placement of the different crops in the bed.** Take into consideration such things as sun/shade and what plants make good neighbors (see Chapter 9). You can make a garden map like the one on the following page.

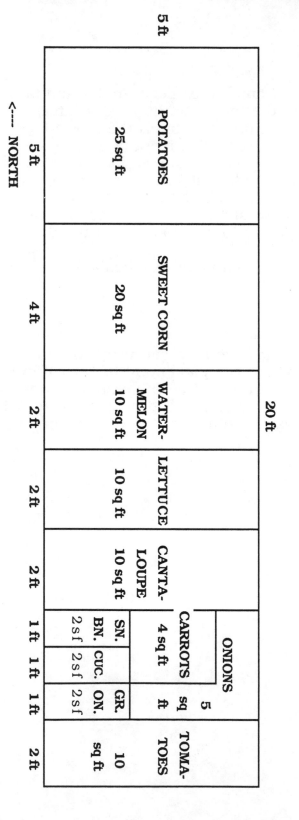

L A Z Y - B E D   G A R D E N   M A P

POTATOES
25 sq ft

SWEET CORN
20 sq ft

WATER-
MELON
10 sq ft

LETTUCE
10 sq ft

CANTA-
LOUPE
10 sq ft

CARROTS
4 sq ft

ONIONS
5 sq ft

SN.
BN.
2sf

CUC.
2sf

GR.
ON.
2sf

TOMA-
TOES
10 sq ft

5 ft

<---- NORTH

5 ft   4 ft   2 ft   2 ft   2 ft   1 ft   1 ft   1 ft   2 ft

20 ft

CHAPTER 9

HOW TO ARRANGE WHAT GOES INTO A LAZY BED:

COMPANION PLANTING

A garden mini-ecosystem is part of a larger ecosystem, interacting with sun, shade, warmth, wind, birds, insects, and animals. Nature's ecosystem is varied and balanced, with harmonious, beneficial interrelationships. While our main focus is on growing a healthy soil, an additional goal is to make our garden **reflect nature's diversity**. Even weeds have a key role to play.

Companion planting involves choosing which crops to put beside each other for the best results, keeping in mind the garden as a whole.

GOOD NEIGHBORS

Although scientific documentation is scarce, gardeners have observed that some plants do better if they are grown with certain other plants. Since plant roots extend over a much wider area than can be observed with the eye, it is possible that plant roots react to each other underground, stimulating or hindering growth. Experienced gardeners have noticed that the crops proposed here for your first lazy bed have the following likes and dislikes when it comes to neighbors. The suggested layout of your lazy bed takes these into account (see Chapter 8).

	Close Neighbors	**Distant Neighbors**
Bush Beans	Potatoes, lettuce, tomatoes	Onions
Carrots	Leaf lettuce, onions, tomatoes	
Corn	Potatoes, beans, cucumbers	
Cucumbers	Beans, corn	Potatoes
Lettuce	Carrots, cucumbers	
Onions	Tomatoes, lettuce	Beans
Potatoes	Beans, corn	Cucumbers, tomatoes
Tomatoes	Onions, carrots	Potatoes

BENEFICIAL INFLUENCES

Following are some plants that have been found by experience to be good for the garden in general. They are perennial, so they might be planted at the end of beds where they will not get in the way of double-digging. Some are herbs that can be enjoyed for tea or seasoning; others are weeds that we would do well to encourage in our gardens instead to trying to get rid of:

Lemon balm (tea)   Oregano (herb)   Dandelion
Chamomile (tea)   Marjoram (herb)   Stinging nettle
Valerian (root is medicinal)

CROP ROTATION

For a number of reasons, it is good not to plant the same crop in the same spot year after year. Different plants take different nutrients, and different quantities of nutrients, out of the soil. Planting the same crop in the same place in succession creates soil nutrient deficiencies and also encourages insect and disease problems.

Compost helps replenish soil nutrients, and planting different crops over time will help to maintain the nutrient balance in the soil. Planting a winter compost crop that includes both grains, with their extensive root systems, and legumes (beans, vetch, clover, and so on), with their nitrogen-fixing ability, will greatly benefit the soil (see Chapter 10).

Compost Crop:
A crop grown to provide material for the compost pile, especially at times when food crops are not being grown. Food crops, such as wheat, can be compost crops as well as food crops. The large amount of straw or stalk also produced is food for the compost pile.

SUN/SHADE

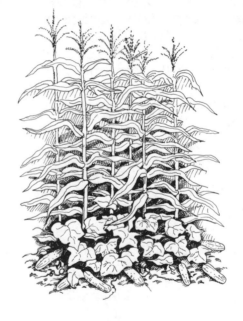

It is easy to forget that tiny seedlings can turn into tall plants. A tall plant, such as corn, can be put where it will shade a plant that enjoys less sun, like peas or potatoes or cucumbers. Sun-loving tomatoes can provide a cooler mini-climate for onions or parsley. Notice that the potatoes in the lazy bed will be shaded by the corn, and the tomatoes will shade the onions, if the bed is oriented as indicated.

Cool weather crops, like lettuce, carrots, onions and potatoes, will do well in partial shade in warmer weather.

ATTRACTING "GOOD BUGS"

Bees and butterflies play an important part in the life cycle of plants, so A garden will benefit if it includes their favorite meals. **Bees can account for up to one-third of the United States crop yield through the pollination they accomplish.** Bees love blue flowers, especially borage and rosemary. Butterflies are attracted to purple, red, yellow and orange flowers and will beautify your garden along with the flowers you plant to attract them.

Other beneficial insects are attracted to the flowers of parsley, dill and cilantro/coriander. Try letting a few of those plants go to seed to serve as feeding stations for helpful insects.

CHAPTER 10

GROWING COMPOST CROPS

We have been focusing on growing food for ourselves, but the only way that the soil can continue to produce food is if we also provide food for the soil -- this provides **sustainable soil fertility**.

A **fertile, healthy soil** will produce **healthy crops** that will keep the **gardener healthy**, too. In order to maintain the fertility of the soil in the garden, the soil must be fed the nutrients it needs to have available for the plants, particularly if we are harvesting the vegetables and eating them without returning our wastes to the soil.

Growing a variety of compost crops provides a diverse mix of food for the microorganisms in the compost pile. These crops may be grown during the cooler season in many climates. If your growing season is very short and your winters are very cold, you will need to grow both a food-crop bed and a compost-crop bed during the warmest months.

	Summer	**Winter**
Cold winter, short summer growing season	Vegetables and compost crops	
Milder winters	Vegetables	Compost crops

You will need to decide how many lazy beds to grow, depending on your climate and your preferences.

One good mixture of compost crops is wheat, cereal rye, fava beans and vetch. The wheat and rye develop extensive root systems that improve the soil structure, while the vetch and fava beans fix nitrogen in the soil. The vetch twines among the taller plants and helps to support them. The straw from the mature wheat and rye plants provides carbon for the compost pile, while the vetch and fava beans, harvested green (at approximately 10% to 50% flower) provide nitrogen. If left to mature fully, the wheat and rye can also provide food for the gardener - in the optimal proportion to allow the phytase in the rye to buffer the phytates in the wheat and rye that would otherwise reduce iron absorption in our bodies from the food we eat.

The compost crop seed recipe per 100 square feet:
> 2 ounces (about 1/3 cup) Hard Red Spring Wheat,
> 0.15 ounce (1-1/2 tsp) Cereal Rye,
> 0.62 ounce (5-1/4 tsp) Vetch, and
> Banner Fava Beans sown on 21-inch centers
> > (about 1-1/2 oz).

Schedule your planting date about 6 weeks before the first hard frost date (Willits, October 4; your area, _____).

You may single-dig your bed (loosen the soil with a spading fork). Or if you are breaking new ground and want optimal yields, you may double-dig the bed if the soil is not too moist.

You can broadcast the wheat, rye and vetch seeds separately and evenly over the bed, and "chop them in" lightly with a rake. The fava beans are then sown on 21-inch offset, or hexagonal, centers. **Be sure the sown seeds are covered with a thin layer of soil equal to the height of the seed when it is lying flat.** Or, for optimal yields, you can sow the seeds in flats and transplant the seedlings into the bed.

VETCH -- (for 100 square feet interplanted) Use Wooly Pod or Winter Hairy Vetch for very cold winter areas, Purple or Common Vetch for warmer areas. When growing vetch only, use 5-1/2 ounces per 100 square feet. When growing vetch with other compost crops, use .62 ounces per 100 square feet. Soak the seed overnight for better germination. Broadcast the seed evenly over the bed, and "chop it in" lightly with a rake.

FAVA BEANS -- (for 100 square feet interplanted) Use Banner Fava Beans, which can take temperatures down to 10°F.

When growing fava beans only, use approximately 18.5 ounces (617 seeds) per 100 square feet, transplanted or sown on 7-inch centers. When growing fava beans with other compost crops, use approximately 1.5 ounces (50 seeds) per 100 square feet, to be transplanted or sown on 21-inch centers. Sow the seeds in flats on 1-inch centers, 10 to 15 days before the scheduled planting date (Willits, September 19 to 24; your area, _____), and transplant when the seedlings are 1 inch high and the roots are about 1 to 2 inches long. Or, sow the seeds directly and cover with a thin layer of soil.

(We recommend transplanting, as Fava Beans establish more completely when they are transplanted.) Use a digging board to distribute your weight evenly.

WHEAT -- (for 100 square feet interplanted) Use Hard Red Spring Wheat. When growing wheat only, use 2-4/10 ounces per 100 square feet. When interplanting with rye, use 2 ounces per 100 square feet. Sow the seeds in flats on 1-inch centers, 5 to 10 days before the scheduled planting date (Willits, September 24 to 29; your area, _____).

(In warmer climates or greenhouses, it can take as few as 5 days for the seed to sprout; in colder climates and outside, it can take as many as 10 days or more.) When the plants are 1 to 1-1/2 inches tall and the roots are 1-1/2 to 2 inches long, transplant on 5-inch centers. If interplanting wheat and rye, transplant 5 wheat plants, then 1 rye plant, and continue throughout the bed. Also, interplant the fava beans on 21-inch centers, either by transplanting or by sowing directly.

RYE -- (for 100 square feet interplanted) Use Cereal Rye *(Secale cereale).* When growing rye only, use .9 ounces per 100 square feet. When interplanting with wheat, use .15 ounces per 100 square feet.
Sow the seeds in flats on 1-inch centers, 5 to 10 days before the scheduled planting date (Willits, September 24 to 29; your area, _____). Transplant after every fifth wheat plant (on 5-inch centers).

GRAZING

Compost crops will need to be cut back, or "grazed", whenever they reach 18 inches high, depending on the weather. This is done so the wind, rain and snow will not cause them to fall over, or "lodge". They may need to be "grazed" two to three times during the winter. Cut them back to 1 inch above the soil, and use the material for your compost pile. Do not graze later than three months before warmer weather (Willits, February 1; your area, _____); the crops need the following 4 months to fully mature and produce seed. In Willits, we usually "graze" these crops about December 1 and February 1, but it varies a lot from year to year.

HARVEST

Compost crops may be ready to harvest as early as May 1, depending on your climate. When the fava beans and vetch are

86

in approximately 50% flower, *carefully* pull out only the fava beans and vetch (the vetch will pull out easily enough; try to get the fava beans out by snapping, pulling or cutting them and without disturbing the wheat and the rye), and use this material in your compost pile. The wheat and rye should continue to mature until the plants are approximately 85% golden and the seed grain is crunchy, about June 1. If seed has set (wheat sometimes does not set seed in winter), thresh the grain while the heads are still attached, or cut off the heads and clean the seed. (See Chapter 12.) Use the straw for your compost pile; be sure to incorporate green material, such as green weeds, green grass (or even comfrey or alfalfa). along with it,

It is also possible that you will have to harvest your compost crops before they are mature, in order to get your bed ready for the expected planting day (Willits, May 21; your area, _____). If so, cut everything off at ground level and use the material for your compost pile. Then double-dig the bed and add compost before you transplant your vegetable or calorie crop seedlings.

Other possibilities for compost crops are clover, oats and agricultural mustard. Bountiful Gardens (see Chapter 4 for address) carries these compost-crop seeds and many others.

CHAPTER 11

KEEPING THE GARDEN HEALTHY

Beginning gardeners are often inclined to worry about getting rid insects and weeds, but it is much more enjoyable to think of insects and weeds as part of Nature's contribution to a diverse ecosystem. Weeds that compete with the plants we are trying to grow should obviously be taken out and added to the compost pile, and insects that insist on helping themselves to our garden vegetables need to be related with gently yet firmly. Generally, a garden will better benefit from the gardener's focus on health and life rather than on death and disease.

A thriving, diverse garden with healthy soil will attract beneficial insects that will make themselves useful pollinating, cleaning up rotting debris, and eating harmful insect larvae. In fact, in a balanced mini-ecosystem, for every seven or eight good bugs, there will be only one harmful one. If we get rid of all the bad bugs in our garden, the good bugs have less to eat and have no reason to stay around to help.

Insects and disease are most likely to attack sick plants, those that are under stress for some reason. Making sure the soil has all the nutrients, soil air, soil moisture and cured compost needed by the plants we are growing is a much better way to use our energy than looking for ways to get rid of pests. Compost made from a variety of plant materials will encourage a variety of microorganisms in the soil, and they will provide the wide range of nutrients and microorganisms needed for healthy plants. Careful transplanting also helps to promote uninterrupted root growth and encourages vigorous, healthy plants. The right amount of water throughout the plants' growing period will also reduce the likelihood of stress.

THE FOUR BASIC KINDS
OF INSECTS
AND
HOW TO CONTROL
THEM EASILY

Chewing or biting, soft-bodied
Chewing or biting, hard-bodied

Aromatic and distasteful sprays, such as garlic, onion and pepper spray

Sucking, soft-bodied

Soap solution sprays (not detergents)

Sucking, hard-bodied

Hand picking

Garlic/Onion Tea Insect Repellent

Mash 10 cloves of garlic or a medium onion. Mix with 2 quarts/litres of water. Let it sit. Strain. Spray without diluting. (Good against nematodes.)

"The Bomb" Insecticide

Melt 1/2 bar of bath soap (not detergent) in 8 quarts/litres of water. Spray. For strong pests, add 2 teaspoons of salt and about 30 mashed cayenne peppers.

CHAPTER 12

GROWING MORE CALORIES

Vegetables provide **important vitamins and minerals** in our diet, but many of them can be considered 'green water' in terms of the energy that they provide. **Our bodies also need calories for energy.** This book has already introduced you to two good calorie crops: potatoes and onions. You may want to consider growing some others.

If you live in a climate (not too cold and not too hot) which will allow you to grow **grains** easily, you can grow these **calorie crops during** the cooler **winter** months in a second lazy bed. For garden fertility, you can also grow **summer compost crops** in the bed -- **corn** or **buckwheat**, for example -- during the warm months. These may also produce a significant yield of grain high in calories.

In addition to grains, **dry beans** are a crop with a lot of calories per pound. However, **grain and bean caloric yields per unit of area are low in comparison with those of potatoes.** (See the discussion in Chapter 2.) Dry beans need to be grown during warm weather. In the garden space that grows dry beans during the warm summer, you can also grow interplanted compost crops, such as wheat and vetch, during the winter.

PLANNING YOUR CALORIE CROPS

The Calorie Crop Map below shows one 100-square-foot calorie crop bed through the year. One-half of the bed will grow dry beans during the main growing season and compost crops during the cool weather. The other half will grow winter grains during the latter part of the cool weather and the beginning of the warm weather, summer compost crops during the rest of the warm weather, and interplanted winter compost crops during the first part of the cool weather. The dates given below are for the Willits climate. You will need to adjust them for your climate.

When you plant these crops for the second year, be sure to **rotate** the oats and wheat **crops** to the previous year's dry bean section, and vice versa.

CALORIE CROP MAP (100 square feet)

(Progression of the growing bed through the seasons)

Main Growing Season	**Summer Compost Crops** 50 sq ft July 15 to Sept. 30	**Dry Beans** 50 sq ft May 21 to Sept. 30

	Winter Compost Crops	
Cool Weather Season	50 sq ft Oct. 1 to Jan. 30	50 sq ft Oct. 1 to May 21

Wheat 25 sq ft	**Oats** 25 sq ft	**Winter Compost Crops** (continued)	5 ft
Feb. 1 to July 14		50 sq ft	
5 ft	5 ft	10 ft	

Refer to the Master Chart in Chapter 8 for details on the following crops.

THE GRAIN SECTION OF THE CALORIE-CROP LAZY BED

The wheat and oats will be transplanted on approximately February 1 in the Willits area (your area, _____). See WINTER COMPOST CROPS, below, for how to prepare the bed.

WHEAT (for 100 square feet):
Growing Instructions: **Use** Hard Red Spring Wheat, 2.4 ounces (slightly rounded 1/3 cup) per 100 square feet (Col. BB) or .6 ounce **(1 tablespoon + 1 teaspoon) for 25 square feet** (2.4 oz x 25 sq ft/100 = .6). On 5-inch centers (Col. CC), a 100-square-foot bed can hold up to 833 plants (Col. DD), so a 25-square-foot area will hold a maximum of 208 plants (833 plants x 25 sq ft/100 = 208.25). To ensure 208 wheat seedlings to transplant, you will need to sow 297 wheat seeds (208 ÷ .70 germination rate [Col. AA] = 297.1). 297 seeds on 1-inch centers (Col. FF) will take up about 1-1/5 standard flats (297 ÷ 250 [see note for Col. GG] = 1.188). (Or you can use Col. GG which is already adjusted for the germination rate: 208 ÷ 175 = 1.18.) Therefore, 1 to 2 weeks (Col. HH) before the expected planting date (Willits, January 15 to 21; your area, _____), **sow** the seed on **1-inch centers** (Col. FF) in approximately **1-1/5 flats** (Col. EE and above calculation). (In a warmer climate or a greenhouse, it can take as few as 5 days for the seed to sprout; in a colder climate and outside, it can take as many as 10 days or more.) **When the plants are 1 to 1-1/2 inches tall and the roots are 1-1/2 to 2 inches long, transplant** on **5-inch centers** (Col. CC) into 25 square feet of the bed.

Harvest when the plants are dry and the seeds are crunchy when you bite one between your teeth (Willits, approximately mid-July; your area, _____). Cut the plants off at ground level. If you know someone who has a mechanical thresher, leave the heads on the stalks -- it is easier to thresh the heads that way. If you will be threshing by hand, cut the heads off the stalks. Let them both dry thoroughly. Use the stalks with other green material for your compost pile.

Thresh the heads by spreading them out on a clean cement floor or driveway (preferably with a rough surface), putting on some clean tennis shoes (preferably with soles that are not too smooth), and doing the shuffle! When the grain has been loosened from the chaff, use two bowls or buckets and pour the grain back and forth between them outside in a stiff wind or with the air from the back end of a vacuum cleaner blowing on them, to separate the chaff from the grain. Store the grain in a clean glass jar. You can cook the wheat berries like rice for supper, or cook them a little longer for breakfast cereal.

OATS: (25 square feet)

Growing Instructions: **Use** Hull-less Oats, 3.5 ounces (2/3 cup) per 100 square feet (Col. BB) or .87 ounce **(2 slightly rounded tablespoons) for 25 square feet** (3.5 oz x 25 sq ft/100 = .875). On 5-inch centers (Col. CC), a 100-square-foot bed can hold up to 833 plants (Col. DD), so a 25-square-foot area will hold a maximum of 208 plants (833 plants x 25 sq ft/100 = 208.25). To ensure 208 oat seedlings to transplant, you will need to sow 297 oat seeds (208 ÷ .70 germination rate [Col. AA] = 297.1). 297 seeds on 1-inch centers (Col. FF) will take up about 1-1/5 standard flats (297 ÷ 250 [see note for Col. GG] = 1.188). (Or you can use Col. GG which is already adjusted for the germination rate: 208 ÷ 175 = 1.18.) Therefore, 1 to 2 weeks (Col. HH) before the expected planting date (Willits, January 15 to 21; your area, _____), **sow** the seed on **1-inch centers** (Col. FF) in approximately **1-1/5 flats** (Col. EE and above calculation). (In a warmer climate or a greenhouse, it can take as few as 5 days for the seed to sprout; in a colder climate and outside, it can take as many as 10 days or more.) **When the plants are 1 to 1-1/2 inches tall and the roots are 1-1/2 to 2 inches long**, **transplant** on **5-inch centers** (Col. CC) into 25 square feet of the bed.

Harvest when the plants are dry and the seeds are crunchy when you bite one between your teeth (Willits, approximately mid-July; your area, _____). Use the same procedure as for wheat.

Thresh as for wheat.

SUMMER COMPOST CROPS: After the grains have been harvested, double-dig that portion of the bed and plant a 60-day corn in 25 square feet and buckwheat in the other 25 square feet.

• CORN FOR COMPOST: (25 square feet)
Use a 60-day corn variety (for example, Montana Bantam; see Chapter 4) planted on 12-inch centers. This is closer than you would plant corn for eating, so you will probably harvest only a few developed ears to eat, but the purpose of this section is to grow material for the compost pile.

Growing Instructions: Use approximately 2.1 ounces (1/3 cup) of seed per 100 square feet (Col. BB) or .52 ounce **(1-1/2 tablespoons) for 25 square feet** (2.1 oz x 25 sq ft/100 = .525). On 12-inch centers (Col. CC), a 100-square-foot bed will hold up to 159 plants, so a 25-square-foot area will hold a maximum of 40 plants (159 plants x 25 sq ft/100 = 39.88). To ensure 40 corn seedlings to transplant, you will need to sow 53 corn seeds (40 ÷ .75 germination rate [Col. AA] = 53.33). 53 seeds on 1-inch centers (Col. FF) will take up approximately 1/5 of a standard flat (53 ÷ 250 [see note for Col. GG] = .212). (Or you can use Col. GG which is already adjusted for the germination rate: 40 ÷ 187 = .213.) Therefore, 2 weeks (Col. HH) before the expected planting date (Willits, July 15; your area, _____), **sow the seed** on **1-inch centers in 1/5 of a flat** (Col. EE). **When the seedlings are about 1 inch tall, transplant** them into the bed on **12-inch centers** (Col. CC), taking care to keep the root as vertical as possible.

Harvest the ears (if there are any) when they are developed (see Chapter 8) and pull the stalks out when they are as dry as possible, to use for the compost pile. In any case, you will need to get the bed ready for the winter compost crops to go in (Willits, about October 1; your area, _____).

• **BUCKWHEAT** (25 square feet): Buckwheat does not have the extensive root system that grain crops do, and it does not fix nitrogen in the soil like beans do, but it is a valuable summer compost crop. It grows quickly and protects the soil during the heat of the summer, and its flowers attract a variety of beneficial insects to your garden. Though it can be grown for buckwheat seeds, this crop is being grown as a compost crop, which also concentrates nitrogen in its body for use in the compost pile.

<u>Growing instructions</u>: **Use** 2.6 ounces (1 cup) of seed for 100 square feet or .65 ounce **(1/4 cup) for 25 square feet**. **Broadcast** the seed evenly over the surface of the soil, then **chop it in** with a rake, using an up-and-down motion.

Harvest the buckwheat by cutting it off at ground level at the end of your growing season. Add the green material to the compost pile.

WINTER COMPOST CROPS: The whole bed may be planted with winter compost crops at the same time, after both the dry beans and the summer compost have been harvested. See Chapter 10 for how to grow the winter compost crops. The compost crops in this 50-square-foot section will need to be pulled out with the roots in order to prepare the 50 square feet where you will plant your wheat and oats. Single-dig this area. If the weather has been wet, you can cover this section of the bed with plastic 1 week before you expect to transplant the wheat and oats, so that it is not too wet to work with.

THE DRY BEAN SECTION OF THE BED

DRY BEANS: (50 square feet)
<u>Growing Instructions</u>: **Use** 12.7 ounces (2-1/4 cups) per 100 square feet (Col. BB)

or 6.4 ounces **(1 slightly rounded cup) for 50 square feet** (12.7 oz x 50 sq ft/100 = 6.35). On 6-inch centers (Col. CC), a 100-square-foot bed can hold up to 621 plants (Col. DD), so a 50-square-foot area will hold a maximum of 310 plants (621 plants x 50 sq ft/100 = 310.5). To ensure 310 dry bean seedlings to transplant, you will need to sow 443 dry bean seeds (310 ÷ .70 germination rate [Col. AA] = 442.8). 442 seeds on 1-inch centers (Col. FF) will take up about 1-3/4 standard flats (442 ÷ 250 [see note for Col. GG] = 1.76). (Or you can use Col. GG which is already adjusted for the germination rate: 310 ÷ 177 = 1.77.) Therefore, 1 to 2 weeks (Col. HH) before the expected planting date (Willits, May 7 to 14; your area, _____), **sow** the seed on **1-inch centers** (Col. FF) in approximately **1-1/5 flats** (Col. EE and above calculation). (In a warmer climate or a greenhouse, it can take as few as 5 days for the seed to sprout; in a colder climate and outside, it can take as many as 10 days or more.) On or near the expected planting day (Willits, May 21; your area, _____), **when the bean seedlings have 2 to 3 true leaves** (in addition to the cotyledons, or seed leaves, **transplant** them on **6-inch centers** (Col. CC) into 50 square feet of the bed, setting the plants in up to the cotyledons.

Harvest: For maximum yields, harvest the beans at the shell-bean stage, when the beans are swollen in the pods but the pods are still green or just starting to dry, and let the beans dry; this way they will be less likely to have weevils, and the plant may produce more flowers and beans. This will allow you to have dry beans without waiting the extra month for the beans to dry on the bush. Or, you may let them dry on the plant and harvest the plants when most of the beans are dry; this involves less handling but more possibility of weevils and a lower yield.

WINTER COMPOST CROPS: The whole bed (100 square feet) may be planted with winter compost crops, after both the dry beans and the summer compost crops have been harvested. See Chapter 10 for how to grow winter compost crops. The winter compost crops in this 50-square-foot section will remain in the bed until this section is double-dug in the spring.

CHAPTER 13

SUPPLIES AND RESOURCES

CATALOGS

In addition to the seed **catalogs** listed in Chapter 4, we would like to suggest a few others worth browsing through **for supplies**:

Bountiful Gardens, 18001 Shafer Ranch Road, Willits CA 95490
    Tools, books and other useful items.

Peaceful Valley Farm Supply, P.O. Box 2209, Grass Valley CA 95945
    Tools and supplies for organic farming and gardening.

Walt Nicke's Garden Talk, P.O. Box 433, Topsfield MA 01983
    Useful products, hints and articles.

Suttons Seeds, London Road, Earley, Reading, Berkshire RG6 1AB, ENGLAND

BOOKS

Some of these books may be out of print, but your local library may have them or be able to get them for you through inter-library loan, or you may be able to find them at a used book store.

Vilmorin Andrieux, M. M. *The Vegetable Garden.* Reprint of 1885 English edition by Ten Speed Press, 1981.
    Developed by the original French intensive gardeners and added to by their English counterparts. For detailed crop descriptions and growing instructions, some of the best ever written. Beautiful engravings of many varieties.

Park's Success With Seeds. Greenwood, SC: Geo. W. Park Seed Co, 1978.

The Organic Gardener's Handbook of Natural Insect and Disease Control. Emmaus, PA: Rodale, 1992.

Hart, Rhonda Massingham. *Bugs, Slugs and Other Thugs: Controlling Garden Pests Organically.* Pownal, VT: Storey Communications, Inc., 1991.

ECOLOGY ACTION PUBLICATIONS

Jeavons, John. *How to Grow More Vegetables.* 4th ed. Berkeley: 10 Speed Press, 1991.

Jeavons, John; Griffin, J. Mogador; and Leler, Robin. *The Backyard Homestead.* Berkeley: 10 Speed Press, 1983.

Duhon, David, and Gebhard, Cindy. *One Circle.* Willits: Ecology Action, 1986.

Jeavons, John. *Booklet 14: The Complete 21-Bed Mini-Farm.* Willits: Ecology Action, 1986.

Cox, Carol, and Staff. *Booklet 26: Learning to Grow All Your Own Food.* Willits: Ecology Action, 1991.

Donelan, Peter. *Booklet 13: Growing to Seed.* Willits: Ecology Action, 1986.

Lazy-Bed Gardener Starter Sets

Here are generous portions of seeds for all the vegetables for your lazy bed (except seed potatoes which can be ordered directly from Ronniger's or purchased from your local nursery), as well as an option for some very helpful tools. The seeds are from Ecology Action's own Bountiful Gardens catalog and are some of the finest varieties available anywhere.

The seeds in this collection are:

Heirloom quality: the kind of seed you would save for your children and grandchildren;

Open-pollinated: so you can save seeds from the crops you grow, if you wish;

Completely untreated: guaranteed to be fresh, vital, and ready for your garden.

Each of the seed packets contains enough or more than enough seed to plant the area recommended in this book and complete directions on how, where, and when to plant are included.

Heirloom Garden Vegetable Seed Collection

Derby Snap Bean	Nantes Carrots, Tip Top
Golden Bantam Corn	Straight Nine Cucumber
Bronze Arrow Lettuce	Haogen Melon
Rutgers Tomato	Southport White Globe Onion
Sugar Baby Watermelon	White Lisbon Onion (green onion)

Compost Crop Seed Collection

Hard Red Spring Wheat	Banner Fava Beans
Cereal Rye	Purple Vetch

Calorie Crop Seed Collection

Hard Red Spring Wheat	Hull-less Oats
Cranberry Dry Bean	

Bountiful Gardens has also put together two collections of tools for the beginning gardener.

Basic Garden Tools

Redwood Seed Flat Kit -- Easy to build! Pre-cut, drilled redwood, nails, and directions for one standard 3-inch-deep flat (14" x 23").

Transplanting Trowel -- Good for moving larger seedlings and for general cultivation. Narrow for better control.

Widger -- The British have developed the perfect tool for moving tiny or small seedlings. Special shape is ideal.

Haws-type Watering Can -- Made of strong, lightweight plastic. Fine head gives a gentle rain of water. Balanced.

D-Handled Spade and Fork

Quality wood D-handled spade and fork that stand up well to double-digging.

See the Bountiful Gardens catalog for watering fans, 6-inch-deep flats, shade-netting and other garden supplies.

Please send order and catalog requests to:

Bountiful Gardens/Ecology Action
18001 Shafer Ranch Road
Willits, CA 95490   Telephone: (707) 459-6410
All prices are postage paid:

____ **Vegetable Seed Collection $ 11.00**
____ **Compost Crop Seed Collection $ 7.00**
____ **Calorie Crop Seed Collection $ 3.50**
____ **Basic Garden Tools $ 31.50**
____ **D-Handled Spade and Fork $ 86.00**
____ *Lazy-Bed Gardening* $ 10.95

_____ Subtotal

_____ California residents add 7.25% sales tax
          for **tools and books**

_____ TOTAL

Payment: __ Check, Money Order (US$ only)

__ Visa __ Mastercard __ American Express

Credit Card No._____

Signature_____ Expires_____
If gift, give name and greeting:

____ **Send FREE Bountiful Gardens Catalog**

Name_____
Address_____
City/State _____Zip_____
Telehone ( ) _____

APPENDIX

As you get more into gardening, it is a good idea to gather helpful data for your garden site. A rain gauge and a good min/max (minimum/maximum temperature) thermometer from your gardening store will allow you to keep records of precipitation and temperatures. These will enable you better understand the gardening year.

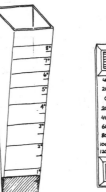 

Rain gauge

Min-max thermometer

SOIL:

1. Type:_____
    (clay, clay-loam, sand, and so on)

2. Soil Test Report attached.

A soil test can be cost-effective if you have five or more beds. We recommend that you have both the Basic and the Trace Mineral Analysis done. Our favorite soil-testing service is Timberleaf Soil Testing Service, 5569 State Street, Albany, OH 45710. Write for instructions and a test-sample kit.

3. Age of growing area (how long site has been used for a garden): _____

4. Size of growing area: _____

5. Growing area faces: _____ (direction, e.g., SSW)

6. Slope of growing area: _____ (flat, rolling, steep, very steep)

CLIMATE:

1. Average Monthly Minimum/Maximum Temperatures

January   ____ / ____   July   ____ / ____

February   ____ / ____   August   ____ / ____

March   ____ / ____   September   ____ / ____

April   ____ / ____   October   ____ / ____

May   ____ / ____   November   ____ / ____

June   ____ / ____   December   ____ / ____

2. Average Monthly Precipitation

January   _____   July   _____

February   _____   August   _____

March   _____   September   _____

April   _____   October   _____

May   _____   November   _____

June   _____   December   _____

KEEPING RECORDS

Make two copies of the forms on the following pages. Use one for precipitation and the other for minimum/maximum temperatures (low temperature / high temperature). If you photocopy the forms on 8-1/2" x 11" paper, you can put them in a 3-ring binder with your other garden records. See *Backyard Homestead* for more planning information.

PRECIPITATION / TEMPERATURES

JANUARY	FEBRUARY	MARCH
1 _____	1 _____	1 _____
2 _____	2 _____	2 _____
3 _____	3 _____	3 _____
4 _____	4 _____	4 _____
5 _____	5 _____	5 _____
6 _____	6 _____	6 _____
7 _____	7 _____	7 _____
8 _____	8 _____	8 _____
9 _____	9 _____	9 _____
10 _____	10 _____	10 _____
11 _____	11 _____	11 _____
12 _____	12 _____	12 _____
13 _____	13 _____	13 _____
14 _____	14 _____	14 _____
15 _____	15 _____	15 _____
16 _____	16 _____	16 _____
17 _____	17 _____	17 _____
18 _____	18 _____	18 _____
19 _____	19 _____	19 _____
20 _____	20 _____	20 _____
21 _____	21 _____	21 _____
22 _____	22 _____	22 _____
23 _____	23 _____	23 _____
24 _____	23 _____	24 _____
25 _____	25 _____	25 _____
26 _____	26 _____	26 _____
27 _____	27 _____	27 _____
28 _____	28 _____	28 _____
29 _____	29 _____	29 _____
30 _____		30 _____
31 _____		31 _____

APRIL

1 _____
2 _____
3 _____
4 _____
5 _____
6 _____
7 _____
8 _____
9 _____
10 _____
11 _____
12 _____
13 _____
14 _____
15 _____
16 _____
17 _____
18 _____
19 _____
20 _____
21 _____
22 _____
23 _____
24 _____
25 _____
26 _____
27 _____
28 _____
29 _____
30 _____

MAY

1 _____
2 _____
3 _____
4 _____
5 _____
6 _____
7 _____
8 _____
9 _____
10 _____
11 _____
12 _____
13 _____
14 _____
15 _____
16 _____
17 _____
18 _____
19 _____
20 _____
21 _____
22 _____
23 _____
23 _____
25 _____
26 _____
27 _____
28 _____
29 _____
30 _____
31 _____

JUNE

1 _____
2 _____
3 _____
4 _____
5 _____
6 _____
7 _____
8 _____
9 _____
10 _____
11 _____
12 _____
13 _____
14 _____
15 _____
16 _____
17 _____
18 _____
19 _____
20 _____
21 _____
22 _____
23 _____
24 _____
25 _____
26 _____
27 _____
28 _____
29 _____
30 _____

JULY	AUGUST	SEPTEMBER
1 _____	1 _____	1 _____
2 _____	2 _____	2 _____
3 _____	3 _____	3 _____
4 _____	4 _____	4 _____
5 _____	5 _____	5 _____
6 _____	6 _____	6 _____
7 _____	7 _____	7 _____
8 _____	8 _____	8 _____
9 _____	9 _____	9 _____
10 _____	10 _____	10 _____
11 _____	11 _____	11 _____
12 _____	12 _____	12 _____
13 _____	13 _____	13 _____
14 _____	14 _____	14 _____
15 _____	15 _____	15 _____
16 _____	16 _____	16 _____
17 _____	17 _____	17 _____
18 _____	18 _____	18 _____
19 _____	19 _____	19 _____
20 _____	20 _____	20 _____
21 _____	21 _____	21 _____
22 _____	22 _____	22 _____
23 _____	23 _____	23 _____
24 _____	23 _____	24 _____
25 _____	25 _____	25 _____
26 _____	26 _____	26 _____
27 _____	27 _____	27 _____
28 _____	28 _____	28 _____
29 _____	29 _____	29 _____
30 _____	30 _____	30 _____
31 _____	31 _____	

OCTOBER	NOVEMBER	DECEMBER
1 _____	1 _____	1 _____
2 _____	2 _____	2 _____
3 _____	3 _____	3 _____
4 _____	4 _____	4 _____
5 _____	5 _____	5 _____
6 _____	6 _____	6 _____
7 _____	7 _____	7 _____
8 _____	8 _____	8 _____
9 _____	9 _____	9 _____
10 _____	10 _____	10 _____
11 _____	11 _____	11 _____
12 _____	12 _____	12 _____
13 _____	13 _____	13 _____
14 _____	14 _____	14 _____
15 _____	15 _____	15 _____
16 _____	16 _____	16 _____
17 _____	17 _____	17 _____
18 _____	18 _____	18 _____
19 _____	19 _____	19 _____
20 _____	20 _____	20 _____
21 _____	21 _____	21 _____
22 _____	22 _____	22 _____
23 _____	23 _____	23 _____
24 _____	23 _____	24 _____
25 _____	25 _____	25 _____
26 _____	26 _____	26 _____
27 _____	27 _____	27 _____
28 _____	28 _____	28 _____
29 _____	29 _____	29 _____
30 _____	30 _____	30 _____
31 _____		31 _____

NOTES

NOTES

NOTES

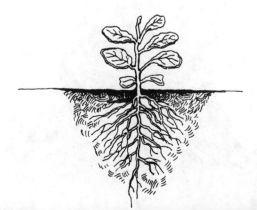

NOTES

NOTES

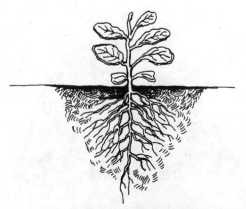

NOTES

NOTES

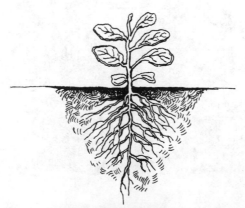

NOTES